SYMPOSIA OF THE
SOCIETY FOR THE STUDY OF HUMAN BIOLOGY

Volume XIX

DEMOGRAPHIC PATTERNS
IN DEVELOPED SOCIETIES

Edited by
R. W. HIORNS

TAYLOR & FRANCIS LTD
LONDON
1980

First published 1980 by Taylor & Francis Ltd, 10–14 Macklin Street,
London WC2B 5NF

© 1980 Taylor & Francis Ltd

Typeset by Red Lion Setters,
22 Brownlow Mews, London WC1N 2LA
Printed and bound in Great Britain by
Redwood Burn Limited, Trowbridge & Esher

British Library Cataloguing in Publication Data

Demographic patterns in developed societies.
  – (Society for the Study of Human Biology.
Symposia; vol. 19 ISSN 0081-153X).
  1. Population – History
  I. Hiorns, Robert William   II. Series
  301.32′9′1812   HB851

ISBN 0–85066–173–0

CONTENTS

PREFACE

Some ten years have passed since the Society for the Study of Human Biology held a symposium with a demographic theme. Now, instead of the biological aspects of population, we consider the recent changes in demographic patterns in developed societies. At any moment in the course of history of a given population, there will be a degree of fascination with the trends currently in operation. These trends are functions of the complex of factors to which that population may be exposed at that moment. We may reflect that these factors have increased in number and in effect in recent years. An analysis of the resulting patterns may therefore be seen as timely and necessary, even though some changes are as yet incomplete.

The contributions presented in this volume review the demographic patterns of fertility, marriage and mortality with reference to the developed societies, in particular in Western Europe and North America. Not only have the experts been able to provide us with classic expositions of the available material including new and improved sources of data, they have appropriately enhanced their articles by incorporating new methodology while maintaining the historical perspective. Naturally, there must be some delimitation of the topics covered, and migration is not discussed separately but only through its effects upon fertility and mortality. The editor is particularly grateful to the authors for the way they have applied their different skills in their contributions. The resulting degree of integration of demographic thought is well beyond that which he would have dared to expect!

The British Society for Population Studies jointly sponsored with the Society for the Study of Human Biology the symposium at which these papers were presented on 6 January 1978. The editor wishes to thank Professor W. Brass and Mr E. Grebenik and the committees of the two sponsoring societies for their considerable assistance in organizing the meeting. The Social Science Research Council provided a grant without which the team of international speakers could not have been assembled. Sir Maurice Kendall and Mr E. Grebenik acted as Chairmen for the sessions and enriched the proceedings enormously. Grateful thanks are also due to the Dean of the Hospital for Sick Children for permission to use facilities at the Hospital, and to Dr A. J. Boyce and Professor E. J. Clegg for their support and assistance with the detailed arrangements.

ROBERT W. HIORNS
University of Oxford
July 1979

SOME SOCIO-ECONOMIC DIFFERENTIALS IN FERTILITY IN ENGLAND AND WALES

JEAN THOMPSON AND MALCOLM BRITTON

Office of Population Censuses and Surveys, St Catherine's House,
10 Kingsway, London WC2B 6JP

Introduction

The main source of information about the size of families in different population sub-groups has traditionally been the Census, though within the past decade the General Household Survey and *ad hoc* family formation surveys have provided new data sources. Census data have shown the significance of family size differentials with respect to such variables as the socio-economic status of the husband, the education of both husband and wife, and the economic status of the married woman. Surveys, because of their depth of questioning, have been able to examine family size in relation to factors such as religion, income, and the number of children in the wife's and husband's families of origin, as well as contributing to monitoring inter-Censal changes in certain socio-economic differentials. The range of information available from the registration of births has also been extended: for example, information about the place of birth of parents of children born in England and Wales has been recorded at birth registration since April 1969; and for each of the years since 1970 samples of live births occurring in those years have been analysed by the social class of the father.

In examining the 1961 Census data for England and Wales, Glass (1968; 1970) found that the relationship between the family size of married women and socio-economic status (as defined by the occupations of their husbands) had changed. The ratio of the completed family size of manual to non-manual groups, which had been around 1·4:1·0 for those marrying in the 1920s and early 1930s, had

1

fallen to less than 1·2:1·0 for the marriages of the 1940s. In particular, the completed family size of men who were large employers or self-employed professional workers had tended to rise over the period; among semi-skilled and skilled manual workers it had appeared to stabilize at a level lower than for the self-employed professional workers; the lowest levels of family size were recorded for intermediate and junior non-manual workers. The 1961 Census showed that the relationship between family size and education had become U-shaped; it was highest where both husband and wife had left full-time education at a comparatively late age, and also for those who had left before the age of 15 years. Glass stressed the importance of analysing family size by whether the married woman was economically active (gainfully employed) or not. In 1961 economically active married women showed a smaller average family size than for any of the socio-economic categories into which their husbands had been classified.

This paper looks at some of the more recent information on family size differentials yielded by the 1971 Census, and the General Household Survey and registration data in the period 1971 to 1976. The aspects picked out for particular examination are the social group of the husband and wife in combination (where she is working), the terminal age of full-time education, and country of birth of the woman.

It is a valuable discipline to ask what should be the purposes and objectives of this analysis and what ends can it serve. Firstly, the study of differential fertility is one aspect of the attempt to understand social processes in general. This often demands analysis of changes in fertility over time, to answer such questions as whether some previously established hierarchical order of sub-populations is being maintained, or whether there is a widening or narrowing of differentials. However, an important purpose can be served by an empirical approach to the study of differential fertility, probing to find classifications of the population that maximize the variability between sub-groups and minimize variability within them. Lastly, descriptive statistics have an importance of their own. For instance, any systematic differences in fertility are likely to be important facts of life, with implications for planning and the provision of social services.

A further valuable discipline is to bear in mind that the relative sizes of different sub-populations will affect the comparisons that can be made. It will be a rare occasion when it is justifiable to disaggregate the population time and again, only to emerge at the end with a sub-population of negligible size, however remarkable its characteristics.

Before moving on to look at what can be said about differentials it is worth recalling briefly the substantial changes that have occurred in the fertility of England and Wales as a whole over the past 20 years. Period fertility—annual number of live births in relation to the number of women of child-bearing age in that year —increased by nearly 30% in 9 years (1955–64) then fell by nearly 40% in 13 years (1964–77); cohort fertility—defined as the average number of live-born children born to women by the end of their childbearing span of life—on the other hand, may well vary by only half this amplitude. But in general the scale and rapidity of change poses some technical problems for the analysis of fertility differentials.

Social Class Differentials

An article in *Population Trends* (Pearce & Britton, 1977) showed that the distribution of average completed family size for marriages of the 1950s, when analysed by the social class of the father, had maintained the approximate U-shape form which seems to have characterized the marriage cohorts of the 1930s. Preliminary data extracted from the 1971 Census extends information about the relationship between completed family size and social class beyond the conventional analysis according to the occupation of the husband, by giving information about the relationship to the occupation of those married women who were economically active at the time of the Census.

Data are presented in table 1 relating to women who in 1971 were approaching the end of their childbearing span of life; whether defined as women born in the 1930s, or those married around the mid 1950s, they were part of those cohorts of women who experienced the rising fertility of the period 1955–64, and had an average completed family size close to 2·4. The range of variation seen in average family size is considerable: deviations from the overall average of from −13 to +18% by husbands', and from −22 to + 13% by wives', occupation group. It is of interest that an approximate U-shape is seen for both distributions, though with a lower point reached for the wives' occupation groups than for the

Table 1. Index of average family size (AFS) of women, married once only, aged 35–39 in 1971, by occupational grouping of husband and wife; England and Wales.

Social class grouping[a]	Occupation of husband		Occupation of wife	
	Per cent of women	AFS ratio	Per cent of women	AFS ratio
I	7	95	—	80
II	22	93	9	87
IIIN	11	87	18	78
IIIM	40	100	5	83
IV	15	105	15	95
V	5	118	5	113
Economically active	[b]	[b]	52	89
Not economically active	[b]	[b]	48	110
All	100	100[c]	100	100[c]

[a] According to the Classification of Occupations, 1970 (HMSO).
[b] Not applicable.
[c] The overall AFS was 2·38 children born alive in marriage.

Source: 1971 Census, 10% Sample.

husbands' (that is, ignoring the very small group of women in class I occupations).

The general shapes of the distributions of family size which underlie the averages given in table 1 are summarized in table 2 in terms of the incidence of, respectively, childlessness and large families (defined here as being those with four or more children). It can be seen from this that the woman's occupation seems to offer, in some respects, a more systematic basis for differentiating fertility characteristics than does the husband's occupation, with the incidence of childlessness showing a particularly sharp differentiation.

The validity of this general conclusion can be further tested by looking at the distribution of average family size when husbands' and wives' occupation groupings are taken in combination. This results in a complex table. Only the Census is capable of providing adequate numbers of observations to this degree of disaggregation but even so—remembering that the analysis of occupational data is

Table 2.   The distribution of family size[a] for women married once only, aged 35–39 in 1971, by occupational grouping of husband and wife; England and Wales.

Social class	Per cent of families with specified number of children			
	Occupation of husband		Occupation of wife	
	0	4 or more	0	4 or more
I	9	13	20	9
II	9	13	14	11
IIIN	11	11	16	8
IIIM	8	19	15	12
IV	9	22	10	16
V	9	30	5	25
Economically active wife	b	b	13	13
Not economically active wife	b	b	4	23
All	9	18	9	17

[a] Children live-born in marriage.
[b] Not applicable.

Source: 1971 Census, 10% sample.

carried out for only a 10% sample of the population—the numbers turning up in some cells in table 3 are so small that the average family size has too great a sampling error attached to it for it to be used in any analysis.

The first observation to be made is that, with one exception, (husbands in social class V with wives not economically active) the range of variation in the index numbers presented in table 3 occurs within that part covering economically active wives. For each occupational group, leaving aside the very small group of married women with social class I occupations (see table 1) the range of variation down each column is considerably greater than across the rows. That is, if the range is used as a measure of homogeneity, a classification of family size according to the occupation of the husband has a relatively high degree of heterogeneity: a classification of average family size by the occupation of the wife leads to what is arguably a set of fairly homogeneous categories.

Table 3.   Index of average family size[a] for women married once only, aged 35–39 in 1971, by occupational grouping of husband and wife in combination; England and Wales.

Wife's social class	Husband's social class						
	I	II	IIIN	IIIM	IV	V	All
I	87	86	(55)	(65)	(68)	[b]	81
II	91	87	83	87	87	101	87
IIIN	81	78	74	79	78	82	78
IIIM	(74)	72	78	84	88	86	83
IV	92	96	91	95	95	102	95
V	(96)	102	102	113	115	119	113
Economically active wife	87	85	80	90	92	100	89
Not economically active wife	100	100	95	113	119	136	109
All wives	95	93	87	100	105	118	100

[a] Children live-born in marriage.
[b] Not applicable.

Source: 1971 Census, 10% sample.
Note: numbers in brackets are based on fewer than 100 observations.

It is to be noted that a reduction of the occupational grouping for wives to a simple manual/non-manual dichotomy would lose sight of the fact that average family size for women in skilled manual occupations (group IIIM) is much nearer the figures for the non-manual groups than for the remainder of the manual group. However, as was seen in table 1, relatively few wives have occupations classed as IIIM, much the largest numbers occurring in IIIN (skilled non-manual) and IV (semi-skilled manual). Thus, in practice, a simple three-fold stratification of families according to whether the wives are in manual occupations, non-manual, or not economically active, would account for a large part of the variability in family size, at least in the cohort being considered here. This would, on the face of it, offer a classification with less variability within strata than any corresponding grouping of husbands' occupations. All this is worth further examination and development, in the light of further data which can be derived from the 1971 Census.

However powerful the empirical evidence presented in table 3, there should be caution in leaping to a general conclusion that data about married women's occupations could be used as predictors of completed family size. The data that have been considered in this paper look at the occupations a particular cohort of women were following at the age at which their family size was complete, or very nearly so. These data cannot convincingly answer a charge that family size may, to some extent, determine occupation, an issue which requires the study of occupational mobility in relation to family circumstances. For instance, although around 50% of all married women were economically active at age 35–39, only something like 10% of those with children had what could be called a virtually continuous work history since their marriage; most of those with children had returned to the labour force after having left it for a period while their children were young.

Without some knowledge of the degree to which women may change occupations on their return to the labour market to fit their domestic needs, or because job availability restricts their choice, there is no firm ground for treating the occupational classification used in table 3 as though it were in effect a cultural classification— though it must be admitted that the temptation is there. What is needed to answer the problem posed is longitudinal data about the connection between women's job experience and family formation; some data of this type can be created from retrospective surveys though, as always in longitudinal analysis, prospective surveys would be the preferred instrument. There appears to be a promising field here for re-analysing some of the surveys of the recent past which collected data on women's employment. Some of the same considerations apply to grouping husbands' occupations and using these as a cultural classification, though as the work history of males is far more likely to be continuous than that of wives the issues raised are not identical.

The analysis of completed family size must be confined to cohorts of women who are effectively at, or near to, the end of childbearing. Differential movements in the period 1971–76 (the period when the rate of decline in fertility was at its most rapid) in numbers of legitimate births according to the occupation of the father as given at birth registration, can give some indication of current trends in family formation. (Corresponding information is not collected at birth registration about the occupation of wives.)

Table 4.   Legitimate live births in 1976 as per cent of those in 1971; England and Wales.

Birth order	Social class of husband				All classes
	I & II	III	IIIM	IV & V	
1	94	73	70	75	77
2	104	81	79	80	85
3	72	72	61	63	65
4 or more	52	41	45	43	45
All orders	91	74	69	69	74
1976: per cent of births of order 4 or more	4	3	8	11	7

Source: Birth registration statistics.

Broad changes for different birth orders within the social class group of the father are given in table 4.

It has to be borne in mind in the interpretation of table 4, that any changes in the numbers at risk in the various social classes would invalidate using changes in numbers of births, as though they also implied changes in fertility rates. However, it emerges pretty clearly that broadly speaking, the halving of the numbers of births of order 4 or higher almost certainly heralds an emerging change of the same magnitude in the distribution of completed families of this size in all social classes (defined by the occupation group of the husband). To this extent, in proportional terms, the differentials in completed family size between the social classes may not be much different at the much lower general level of fertility which has characterized more recent generations, than the differentials shown by the generation of much higher fertility which was considered in earlier sections of this paper.

The changes seen in numbers of first and second births in table 4 are more problematic to interpret. First births in social classes I and II declined in the period 1971–76. Survey evidence suggests that they were already declining before 1971, with non-manual social classes leading off in the later 1960s in the phenomenon of post-ponement of first births after marriage. Numbers of first births

Table 5. Average completed family size[a] (AFS) by terminal age of
full-time education of wife (TAE); England and Wales.

1961[b]			1974–76[c]		
TAE	Per cent of wives	AFS ratio	TAE	Per cent of wives	AFS ratio
Under 15	73	102	15 or less	72	102
15–16	19	94	16–18	20	93
17 or more	8	96	19 or more	8	97
		100			100
		(2·02)			(2·30)

[a] Children born live in current marriage.
[b] Women married once only, married 15–19 years.
[c] Women ages 40–44, AFS in current marriage.

Source: 1961 Census Fertility Tables, General Household Survey
1974–76.

only began to fall sharply after 1971 among social classes where the
husband was in manual occupation; it is worth drawing attention in
this connection to the sharp reduction in the number of pre-maritally
conceived live births as a major factor in this recent phenomenon of
postponement of the start of childbearing in social classes IV and V.

Terminal age of education

The 1961 Census gave information about family size cross-
classified by the terminal age of full-time education (TAE) of both
husband and wife. Interpretation of the data must be qualified by
the great variations in the numbers of people appearing in different
cells of the resulting table: for marriages of 15–19 years duration in
1961, where family size was virtually complete, nearly two-thirds of
couples appeared in the single cell which represented in effect both
husband and wife leaving school at the minimum possible age. The
variations in family size according to terminal age of education
showed some systematic features, ranging from −23 to +6%
around the then national average.

It seems of interest to make a comparison, however limited, of
recent data from the General Household Survey with that from the
1961 Census. Much has changed in patterns of education over this

period and it seemed useful to see whether there were any connections with changes in fertility.

The data presented in table 5 are of interest as much for a methodological as a substantive argument. Terminal age of full-time
education is a hierarchical variable—you have more of it, or less of
it, but it is fixed over the succeeding life-cycle (unlike, to some
extent, social class and economic status which can change both up
and down at any point in the life-cycle). The available figures were
such that class intervals could be defined for corresponding
percentage points in the two distributions of TAE in the cohorts
being compared. The differences in the class boundaries at the two
points of time show clearly how TAE has increased with time. The
variation shown in average family size over the three-fold classification by TAE is not great for either cohort, but what is worth
remarking is the fact that there was the same variation about the
respective means for the two cohorts being studied, even though the
means themselves were very different.

Results from the General Household Survey promise to be of
particular use in trying to identify what social differentials there
have been within the recent phase of steep decline in fertility. By
amalgamating data for marriage cohorts from several years of the

Table 6.   Per cent of wives still childless after 2 exact years of marriage[a] by
husband's social group and terminal age of full-time education (TAE) of wife
in combination; England and Wales.

Husband's occupation	TAE of wife	Period of marriage					
		1960–64		1965–68		1969–71	
		A	B	A	B	A	B
Manual	15 or less	40	(48)	37	(44)	39	(40)
	16 +	46	(12)	46	(14)	54	(19)
Non-manual	15 or less	52	(18)	57	(17)	58	(13)
	16 +	57	(22)	62	(26)	74	(29)
Total		47	(100)	48	(100)	54	(100)

N.B. All figures relate to current marriages of women married under age 30.

[a] Figures in brackets show the percentages of wives in the various categories.

Source: General Household Survey, 1974–76.

Table 7.   Live births to women born in selected countries.

| | Women born in: | | | |
	All countries	Irish Republic	Indian sub-continent	West Indies[a]
Total Period Fertility Rate, 1971	2·38	3·5	5·4	3·4
Number of births in 1976, 1971 = 100 Total	75	53	100	57
Legitimate births by birth order				
1	77	53	119	66
2	85	63	103	72
3	64	50	104	41
4 or more	45	39	83	24

[a] Including Guyana and Belize.

GHS, enough numbers have been generated to allow a broad classi-fication of the husband's occupation (into manual/non-manual groups) by the terminal age of education of the wife. this can, of course, be seen as one aspect of the attempt to probe further for what may lie behind the apparent importance (seen in table 3) of women's occupation as a differentiating factor in fertility. The data presented in table 6 relate to the phenomenon of the postponement of the start of childbearing seen in marriage cohorts of the late 1960s and early 1970s. They establish that in this period, it was the more educated women—those who had in any event a pattern of a later age at the start of childbearing—who postponed yet further the start of their families after marriage; for the marriage cohorts up to those of 1969–71 at least, there was little change in the speed of childbearing for those leaving school at the minimum age. Unfortunately data are, as yet, not available to show what effect the raising of the minimum school leaving age to age 16 may have had both on marriage and on the timing of births.

Country of birth
Information now collected at birth registration gives current data

about differential fertility according to the country of birth of the mother. This information is, however, only available from April 1969; prior to that it was only periodically available, from the Census.

It is of particular interest to consider changes in differentials over the five years 1971 – 76 when fertility in general showed a rapid rate of decline.

Figures are presented in table 7 relating to numbers of births occurring in England and Wales to mothers themselves born in selected overseas countries. In 1971 these selected countries between them accounted for about half of the overseas-born population in this country. This table also shows that the Total Period Fertility Rate (TPFR) for the selected countries was, in 1971, considerably higher than that for all women in England and Wales. (The TPFR measures the average number of live-born children per woman that would result if women survived to the end of their reproductive period, and throughout this period were subject to the age specific fertility rates of the calendar year in question.) The table also shows that between 1971 and 1976 births to mothers born in the Irish Republic and the West Indies each nearly halved in overall number, as compared with a fall of one quarter for England and Wales as a whole; the number of births to women born in the Indian sub-continent, however, showed no change. Looking at the figures for different orders of birth, a particularly big decline is seen in those of order 4 or more for women from the West Indies.

The general inference from table 7 is that for women born in the Irish Republic and the West Indies, declining family sizes would appear to explain declines of the magnitude shown for the higher-order births; the size of the population of women born in the West Indies is estimated to have changed little over the period (*Population Trends*, 1978) and the proportion of larger families thus seems to have fallen particularly rapidly in this population. There was an increase in the size of the population of women born in the Indian sub-continent and this, combined with a fall in births of order 4 or more, points to some modest fall in fertility in this population in the period 1971 – 76 (*Population Trends*, 1978).

On this evidence, there was a shift in the first half of the 1970s in the distribution of differential fertility according to country of birth, in the sense that at least two countries of the three selected ones considered had current fertility in 1971 notably higher than the England and Wales average, but subsequently showed falls greater than the average for England and Wales as a whole; the third group showed a fall in fertility, but smaller than the national average, and in that sense differential fertility in 1976 had a wider range of variation than in 1971.

References

GLASS, D.V., (1968) Fertility trends in Europe since the Second World War. *Population Studies* Vol. XXII, No. 1.

GLASS, D.V. (1970) The components of natural increase in England and Wales. *Supplement to Population Studies*, May 1970.

PEARCE, D. and BRITTON, M.S. (1977), The decline in births: some socio-economic aspects. *Population Trends* No. 7.

POPULATION TRENDS (1978) Marriage and Fertility Patterns in the population of New Commonwealth and Pakistan ethnic origin. *Population Trends* No. 11.

COMPONENTS OF TEMPORAL VARIATIONS IN AMERICAN FERTILITY

NORMAN B. RYDER

Office of Population Research, Princeton University, 21 Prospect Avenue,
Princeton, New Jersey 08540

The purpose of this account is to provide an explanation of the movements of the American birth rate over the past sixty years. The level at which explanation is sought is purely demographic, and the scope of the inquiry is limited to a single set of data †. Such a pedestrian exercise derives its sole justification from a possible increase in the precision with which we can formulate the questions for which answers are required from the substantive disciplines underlying the terrain of mere demography. The main contention of the paper is that inept measurement procedures have misled us into concentrating on the wrong questions. Although the data apply only to the United States, it seems plausible that the configuration of change provoking our difficulties is common at least to all low-fertility societies.

The task of analysis, using that term in its literal sense of decomposition, begins with occurrences of events of interest, and moves backward to the sources, essentially the reverse of how life proceeds. We begin with the outputs and try to divine what the inputs may have been. Thus the problem of calculating the classic fertility rate is to determine the appropriate denominator (of person-years of exposure to risk) to associate with the initial

---

† With obvious minor exceptions, all data used in this paper come from: Heuser, Robert L., *Fertility Tables for Birth Cohorts by Color: United States 1917–73*, (DHEW Publication No. (HRA)76-1152), National Center for Health Statistics, Rockville, Md., April, 1976, together with unpublished extensions for years 1974 and 1975, supplied by Mr Heuser.

observation of a numerator (of births); the experience being studied begins with exposure to risk and the upshot is the occurrence of births. Likewise, at the start of an inquiry we are presented with data collected period by period. These observations are the cross-sectional consequences of the changing performance of the succession of cohorts who move through their lives and provide the inputs to the system. Simply stated, the analysis of the determinants of reproductive behaviour requires the cohort mode of temporal aggregation of data. Studies of temporal variations in fertility which remain locked within the period mode, and thus fail to restore the natural order of things, yield results which mislead us with respect not only to the magnitude and direction of change but also to the dimensions of the reproductive process which are involved.

The dimensions of which we speak in particular are the quantum and tempo of cohort fertility. The term 'quantum' is used to signify measurements associated with the aggregate number of births occurring over the lifetime of a cohort; the term 'tempo' is used to signify measurements associated with the time pattern of those births. The fundamental flaw in research based on the period mode of temporal aggregation is simply that changes in cohort tempo are manifested as changes in period quantum.

The Birth Rate and the Age Distribution Factor

Demographers are restive with the use of this humble measure as an index of fertility, because its variations reflect not only changes in fertility itself, in some deeper sense, but also changes in the age distribution of the population. The latter intrusion is doubly unfortunate: it destroys the purity of the measure by manifesting the influence of the past as well as the present, and thus makes the outcome ill-defined in a temporal sense; and it is affected not only by past fertility but by past mortality and migration as well.

Demographers prefer to work with what is called the period total fertility rate, $F(t)$, the sum, over all ages, of the birth rates for women of each age (see Appendix 1). The influence of the age distribution (not part of the period total fertility rate but certainly part of the crude birth rate) can be measured by the ratio of the birth rate (expressed with the conventional base of one thousand person-years) to the period total fertility rate (per woman). The

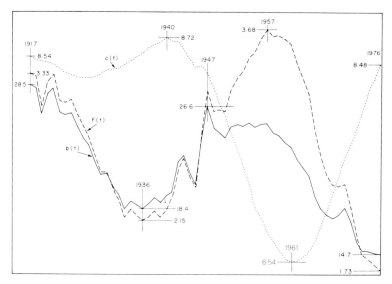

Figure 1.   Crude Birth Rate, $b(t)$; Period Total Fertility Rate, $F(t)$; Age
Distribution Factor, $c(t) = b(t)/F(t)$; USA 1917–76.

result is called the age distribution factor, and is plotted as the
parameter $c(t)$ in figure 1 (see table 1). The birth rate ($b(t)$) is simply
the product of $c(t)$ and the period total fertility rate, $f(t)$. One can
divide the sixty-year span almost precisely in half with respect to
the age distribution factor. Over the first three decades, there
would be little to choose, in a study of temporal variations, between
the birth rate and the total fertility rate, because the age distribution factor changed so little. It is interesting from a standpoint of
the history of demographic methods that the emphasis on the role
of the age distribution in affecting crude rates came into the field
most prominently during a period in which the age distribution, at
least for time series purposes, could have been ignored without
loss.

In the past three decades, on the contrary, there has been a very
wide divergence between the two measures of fertility, associated
with a long decline and then a long rise in the age distribution
factor. Those concerned with the consequences of reproductive
behaviour quite properly focus on the birth rate, or even on the
number of births. If the age distribution factor had remained

Table 1.   The birth rate and the age distribution factor, pp. 1917–76, US.

t	b(t)	F(t)	c(t) = b(t)/F(t)	t	b(t)	F(t)	c(t) = b(t)/F(t)
				1946	24·12	2·8579	8·442
1917	28·47	3·3333	8·540	1947	26·61	3·1812	8·364
1918	28·20	3·3122	8·513	1948	24·90	3·0260	8·227
1919	26·08	3·0677	8·501	1949	24·54	3·0362	8·084
1920	27·71	3·2633	8·491	1950	24·10	3·0280	7·959
1921	28·15	3·3262	8·462	1951	24·92	3·1991	7·789
1922	26·19	3·1094	8·422	1952	25·11	3·2865	7·640
1923	25·99	3·1012	8·382	1953	25·02	3·3494	7·470
1924	26·11	3·1207	8·365	1954	25·26	3·4612	7·298
1925	25·11	3·0116	8·339	1955	24·94	3·4983	7·128
1926	24·18	2·9007	8·337	1956	25·16	3·6047	6·981
1927	23·54	2·8243	8·334	1957	25·24	3·6824	6·854
1928	22·19	2·6598	8·343	1958	24·50	3·6289	6·751
1929	21·20	2·5320	8·374	1959	24·28	3·6382	6·674
1930	21·27	2·5325	8·399	1960	23·74	3·6057	6·585
1931	20·20	2·4017	8·412	1961	23·32	3·5639	6·542
1932	19·55	2·3186	8·430	1962	22·42	3·4233	6·548
1933	18·37	2·1720	8·458	1963	21·71	3·2978	6·587
1934	18·96	2·2320	8·495	1964	21·04	3·1709	6·636
1935	18·68	2·1887	8·535	1965	19·40	2·8816	6·732
1936	18·39	2·1456	8·571	1966	18·41	2·6704	6·894
1937	18·73	2·1733	8·619	1967	17·80	2·5255	7·046
1938	19·23	2·2217	8·654	1968	17·52	2·4310	7·208
1939	18·84	2·1717	8·676	1969	17·83	2·4229	7·359
1940	19·44	2·2290	8·719	1970	18·36	2·4317	7·550
1941	20·26	2·3315	8·691	1971	17·24	2·2454	7·680
1942	22·16	2·5548	8·675	1972	15·65	1·9936	7·848
1943	22·70	2·6402	8·598	1973	14·95	1·8625	8·026
1944	21·24	2·4945	8·513	1974	14·95	1·8244	8·195
1945	20·42	2·4218	8·434	1975	14·75	1·7703	8·334
				1976	14·69	1·7319	8·483

b(t) = Crude birth rate (per 1000 person-years).
F(t) = Period total fertility rate (per woman).
c(t) = Age distribution factor.

constant during the baby boom (the rise of the period total fertility rate from 1936 to 1957) the birth rate would have peaked not at 25·2 (ignoring the spike in the immediate postwar period) but rather at 31·1; instead of the 4·3 million births which occurred in 1957, there would have been 5·3 million. Similarly, had the age distribution factor remained constant from 1957 until the present, the birth rate now would not be 14·7, but rather 11·9, and we would have 20% fewer births.

The sources of movement in the age distribution factor can be identified rather precisely in a population closed to migration (see Appendix 1): (1) the birth rate of a generation ago; (2) the inverse of population growth in the past generation; (3) the proportion of female babies surviving from a generation ago. To give some empirical feel for the relative importance of these factors in the movement of $c(t)$, we note that its peak was in 1940 and its trough in 1961. Between 1940 and 1961, the relevant birth rate fell by 35%, the inverse of growth fell by 8%, and female survival rose by 9%. Thus, the dominant factor in the decline of $c(t)$ was the birth rate of a generation before. Similarly, from 1961 to 1976, the relevant birth rate has risen by 32%, the inverse of growth has risen by 2%, and female survival has risen by 1%. Even more so, the recent rise in $c(t)$ has been dominated by the movement of the birth rate a generation before.

The almost precise counterbalancing of movements of the period total fertility rate by movements of the age distribution factor has played a major role in dampening the outcome in number of births per annum.

It is an interesting question whether these developments should be thought of as fortuitous or intelligible. The size of a cohort relative to its immediate predecessors is probably an important influence on the careers of its members. The society has the problem of assimilating each new cohort in turn, as it reaches a major juncture in its life-cycle. If that problem is exacerbated because the numbers involved are larger than the society has become accustomed to handling, it is not implausible that the members of the cohort will take longer to make the transition, for example into the labour force, into marriage, and into parenthood (Ryder, 1965). The evidence for the United States in the present century suggests a rather strong relationship between relevant variables, although some of this may be attributable to chance.

Without appreciable risk, we can project the movements of the age distribution factor ahead to the year 2000. If the total fertility rate were to remain fixed henceforth, then $c(t)$ would push the birth rate up a little more (by some three or four per cent) over the next five years, but then would begin to operate as a depressant, bringing the birth rate down by about one-third, to a value of 11 in the year 2000. Otherwise said, if we are to avoid a declining birth rate over the rest of the century, then the period total fertility rate must be increased by something like 50% over its present level. The secondary baby boom is almost over (without showing overt effects) and the current trough in fertility—if trough it is—will dominate the movement of the age distribution factor for the next generation.

Distributional Distortion

In this section, we have two key tasks to perform, along the two axes on which this paper is focused—cohort and period, on the one hand, and quantum and tempo, on the other. The first is to distinguish between those movements of period fertility which can properly be ascribed to movements of the cohort quantum parameters, and those which respond to movements of cohort tempo; the second is to translate the process from the period to the cohort mode, for subsequent inter-cohort analysis.

Each cohort has a total fertility rate, which is identically its mean number of births per woman (under the assumption of no mortality before menopause). The total fertility rate can be thought of as distributed over time, with a particular proportion allocated to each year through which the cohort passes in the course of its reproductive life. We have calculated those proportions for each cohort, and re-assembled the results period by period. This calculation, as well as the production of cohort parameters to be described below, has required some projection of fertility for cohorts still within the reproductive age span in the last year of record, 1975. Complete schedules were projected for birth cohorts up to c.1950,† on the assumption that central age−parity-specific birth rates remain fixed henceforth at their 1975 level (see Appendix 2). Scepticism is certainly warranted concerning the results of any assumption about the future, and particularly an assumption of constancy—considering the volatility of fertility in the recent past. The outcome should be regarded not as a forecast, but rather as a

---

† The expression c. 1950 implies the 1950 cohort. Likewise cc. for cohorts.

demonstration of what would happen if the assumption were to hold. To guard against misimpression, as well as to indicate the innocuousness of the assumption, we present at appropriate places below indications of the modifications in our results under the alternative assumption that fertility remains fixed henceforth at 20% above the 1975 level.

There is some information available about events subsequent to 1975. An estimate of the period total fertility rate for 1976 has been published indicating a value 2% lower than that for 1975 (Gibson, 1977). Provisional birth data, in comparison to their counterparts for the preceding year, suggest that the value of the period total fertility rate for 1977 will be approximately 2% higher than that for 1975. Moreover, some of that increase from 1975 to 1977 is attributable to changes in the parity distribution, changes which are allowed for by use of parity-specific fertility rates in the projection.

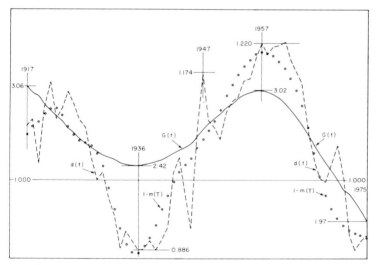

Figure 2. Mean Cohort Total Fertility Rate in Period, $G(t)$; Index of Distributional Distortion, $d(t)$; Translation Multiplier, $1 - m(t)$; USA 1917–75.

The sum for a period of the proportions of its total fertility rate each cohort experiences in that period is labelled in figure 2 as the index of distributional distortion, $d(t)$. Now if every cohort had the same time distribution of fertility, the index would be unity, but in

Table 2.   Distributional distortion. pp. 1917–75, US.

t	$G(t)$	$d(t)$	$1 - m(t)$	$y(t)$
1917	3·0609	1·0890	1·0741	+0·87
1918	3·0155	1·0984	1·0878	+1·16
1919	2·9824	1·0286	1·0953	−5.57
1920	2·9202	1·1175	1·1079	+1·44
1921	2·8706	1·1587	1·1136	+4·13
1922	2·8254	1·1005	1·1150	−3·24
1923	2·7789	1·1160	1·1054	−1·22
1924	2·7303	1·1430	1·0883	+2·11
1925	2·6858	1·1213	1·0740	−0·18
1926	2·6425	1·0877	1·0639	−0·58
1927	2·6023	1·0853	1·0595	+1·55
1928	2·5649	1·0370	1·0555	−0·77
1929	2·5290	1·0012	1·0445	−1·88
1930	2·5005	1·0128	1·0226	+1·43
1931	2·4762	0·9699	0·9894	+0·38
1932	2·4577	0·9434	0·9523	+0·50
1933	2·4415	0·8896	0·9207	−2·82
1934	2·4295	0·9187	0·8958	+1·94
1935	2·4241	0·9029	0·8832	+0·99
1936	2·4217	0·8860	0·8819	−1·60
1937	2·4275	0·8953	0·8917	+0·08
1938	2·4371	0·9116	0·9072	+2·05
1939	2·4514	0·8859	0·9285	−1·03
1940	2·4698	0·9025	0·9520	−1·03
1941	2·4949	0·9345	0·9747	−1·88
1942	2·5233	1·0125	0·9975	+1·61
1943	2·5465	1·0368	1·0122	+4·56
1944	2·5711	0·9702	1·0249	−1·51
1945	2·5959	0·9333	1·0352	−7·47
1946	2·6494	1·0787	1·0510	+2·32
1947	2·7104	1·1737	1·0656	+5·92
1948	2·7576	1·0974	1·0799	−2·35
1949	2·8020	1·0836	1·0952	−1·04
1950	2·8416	1·0656	1·1130	−1·09
1951	2·8865	1·1083	1·1357	+0·92
1952	2·9219	1·1248	1·1539	+0·49
1953	2·9557	1·1332	1·1705	−0·59
1954	2·9838	1·1600	1·1841	+0·62
1955	3·0052	1·1641	1·1942	−0·88
1956	3·0180	1·1944	1·2017	+0·08
1957	3·0186	1·2199	1·2052	+1·14
1958	3·0098	1·2057	1·2049	−0·86
1959	2·9892	1·2171	1·1996	−0·19
1960	2·9589	1·2186	1·1907	+0·09

Table 2.   (continued)

t	$G(t)$	$d(t)$	$1 - m(t)$	$y(t)$
1961	2·9174	1·2216	1·1797	+0·64
1962	2·8640	1·1953	1·1641	−0·66
1963	2·8059	1·1753	1·1456	+0·33
1964	2·7437	1·1557	1·1201	+1·65
1965	2·6714	1·0787	1·0857	−0·89
1966	2·5909	1·0307	1·0430	−0·37
1967	2·5149	1·0042	1·0056	+0·16
1968	2·4403	0·9962	0·9752	−1·51
1969	2·3657	1·0242	0·9530	−0·56
1970	2·3012	1·0567	0·9384	+3·05
1971	2·2360	1·0042	0·9273	+1·59
1972	2·1900	0·9103	0·9199	−2·63
1973	2·1249	0·8765	0·9138	−3·75
1974	2·0497	0·8901	0·9099	−0·34
1975	1·9690	0·8991	0·9063	+2·05

$G(t)$ = Mean cohort total fertility rate for a period ($= F(t)/d(t)$).

$d(t)$ = Index of distributional distortion (sum of proportions of cohort total fertility rates allocated to period t).

$1 - m(t)$ = Translation multiplier (complement of time-derivative of mean age of cohort fertility).

$y(t)$ = Short-term period effect (per cent deviation of $(d(t))/(1 - m(t))$ from 7-term moving quadratic).

fact the tempo changes from cohort to cohort, and the register of those changes is the movement of $d(t)$. In short, it is a measure of change in cohort tempo.

There are two distinct ways in which $d(t)$ changes, as one can see from figure 2. In the first place, there are episodes during which cohorts are having children at progressively younger ages; that implies higher proportions for the earlier older cohorts and higher proportions for the later younger cohorts, in each year during the episode, and thus a substantial positive departure of $d(t)$ from unity. Likewise, there are episodes during which cohorts are having children at progressively older ages, with the opposite effect. This is the essential explanation of the long swings in $d(t)$ from above unity to below unity to above unity to below unity over the 60 years shown. In the second place, some periods will be viewed by all cohorts as relatively favourable to childbearing, in which case the proportions for every cohort (in every age) in such periods will be higher than they otherwise would have been. Likewise, some periods will be viewed by all cohorts as relatively unfavourable to childbearing, with the opposite result. This is the essential explanation of the short-term fluctuations of $d(t)$ around the longer swings. For obvious reasons, these two sources of variations of $d(t)$ are thought of as long-term and short-term effects on period fertility of changes in cohort tempo.

Given an index of the influence of the tempo of cohort fertility on the period-by-period variations, we obtain a measure of the role played by the changes in the quantum of cohort fertility simply by dividing the period total fertility rate (as shown in figure 1) by the index of distributional distortion; the result is labelled $G(t)$ in figure 2. This measure is an average of the fertility of the cohorts contributing to the period in question. More precisely, it is a weighted harmonic mean of the cohort total fertility rates, where the weights are the proportions of the fertility of the period contributed by each cohort (see Appendix 2). These weights are sufficiently close to equal over a considerable age span to approximate a linear moving average based on a large number of terms. The cohort total fertility rate moved first through a trough and then through a peak (see figure 4). A moving average has the property of dampening such swings appreciably. Thus the trough and peak values registered for $G(t)$ are some 6·5% less extreme than those for the cohort series itself.

Looking now at the results in figure 2, we see that there have been two superimposed complete fluctuations which have produced temporal variations in the period total fertility rate. The fluctuation with the smaller amplitude is that reflecting changes in the quantum of cohort fertility; that with the larger amplitude is the influence of changes in the tempo of cohort fertility. More precise quantification of this generalization is attempted in the section on 'allocation of responsibility' below. Part of what is being identified is particular to the era under examination. Were we to push this series back in time, we would find much higher values for $G(t)$. We have a value of 4·07 for the total fertility rate of c.1867 and the values at the beginning of the nineteenth century have been estimated at perhaps twice that level. The index of distributional distortion, on the other hand, is unlikely to have shown more pronounced

swings than those displayed here, except perhaps during the Civil War.
We have spoken of the index of distributional distortion as
having a long-term and a short-term component. Although it
would be possible to distinguish these components by arbitrary
statistical means, our preference is to seek a resolution derivative
from demographic considerations. It has already been suggested
that the long-term swings in this index reflect broad movements of
the age distribution of cohort childbearing. We have provided elsewhere a general mathematical statement of the relationship (Ryder,
1964). The simplest approximation to what is, in general, a
complex situation is that, if the proportions of cohort childbearing
in each age (and thus in each year) were changing linearly over the
contributing cohorts, then the value of the distributional index
would be $(1 - m)$, where m is the annual change in the mean age of
cohort fertility. Accordingly, we have calculated those values and
plotted them in figure 2 as circles. It is apparent that they yield a
smoothed version of the $d(t)$ curve. The root-mean-squared deviation of $(1 - m(t))$ from $d(t)$ is less than 4% of the mean of $d(t)$.
Since $(1 - m(t))$ purports to capture only the long-term movements
of $d(t)$, and leave the short-term deviations aside, such a result is
most encouraging.

A footnote is required on the dating of the values of $(1 - m(t))$.
There is always a problem of displaying cohort results—which
represent experience over a considerable time span—in relation to
period results. The practice we have followed is to identify the
average cohort represented in the period, $T = t - A(t)$, and obtain
an interpolated value of $(1 - m)$ for that cohort. The values of the
time-derivative of the mean age of cohort fertility were obtained by
fitting a seven-term moving quadratic to the series for the mean age
of cohort fertility (see Appendix 2).

We are encouraged by the closeness of fit of $1 - m(t)$ to $d(t)$ to
use the former (reflective of long-term movements in the index) as a
divisor of $d(t)$ to remove its long-term component, and treat the
residual as the short-term deviations. Specifically, we calculated
$d(t)/(1 - m(t))$ and fitted a seven-term moving quadratic to the
resultant ratio. In figure 3, we show the percentage by which the
observation for each individual year deviates from that fitted value,
and label it the short-term period effect. The results are simple to
describe. There are three major fluctuations—at the beginning,

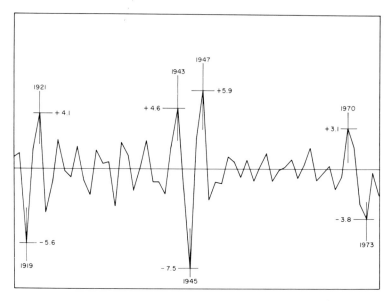

Figure 3.   Short-term Period Effects. [Per cent deviations of $\frac{d(t)}{1 - m(t)}$ from 7-term moving quadratic] USA, 1917–75.

middle and end of the series—and quite a bit of noise in between, although somewhat noisier in the earlier segment than in the later. The three major fluctuations are associated in time with three wars —World War 1, World War 2, and the Vietnam War. That the first two of these wars was influential on fertility is well-known, but the third has not attracted particular attention, and for two interesting reasons. In the first place, if one were relying on the period total fertility rate as one's index of choice, as in figure 1, one would be hard pressed to perceive any more than a temporary interruption of a decline in fertility, over two years, an interruption which would excite little comment because most demographers were looking for signs that the rather unexpected drop in fertility was coming to a halt. Now one does see the fluctuation vividly in an examination of the more detailed fertility rates specific for age and parity but it so happened that, subsequent to the publication of those detailed rates for 1968, there was a long hiatus before the subsequent years' results came out, and a major event in American fertility was unwittingly concealed.

Two questions arise concerning the Vietnam War fluctuation. In the first place, the part of the $d(t)$ series and $(1 - m(t))$ series being used for these calculations are the most highly estimated, and thus the most prone to error of assumption. Nevertheless, what is being shown is a comparison of values for successive cohorts; our inference would be mistaken only if there were a substantial and unprecedented irregularity in the sequence of cohort total fertility rates. Furthermore, if we had used, say, higher estimates of completed fertility for the cohorts now in the childbearing ages, we would have deflated, by approximately equal proportions, both the value for $d(t)$ and the value for $(1 - m(t))$, leaving the ratio essentially unchanged.

The second question concerns the measurement of the impact of the war. As a simple indicator, we have calculated the size of the population classified as 'armed forces abroad'. In thousands, the numbers for 1917–1919 were 148, 1 357, and 551 respectively; the numbers for 1941–46 were 248, 940, 2 454, 5 512, 7 447, and 1 335 respectively; and for 1965–72, they were 765, 985, 1 255, 1 305, 1 295, 1 058, 833, and 612 respectively. What gave the Vietnam War its substantial impact on fertility was not so much the magnitude of involvement in any one year as the circumstance that it lasted so long. For example, the numbers of armed forces abroad during the Korean War were comparable in magnitude to the annual numbers during the Vietnam War, but the impact on fertility was negligible because of the short duration of that conflict (from mid-1950 to early 1952). Moreover, the impact of the Vietnam War was by no means restricted to those who served overseas; many others must have had their family formation plans disrupted by the uncertainty associated with the draft.

Some interest has been expressed in the possible economic correlates of short-term variations in fertility. In our view, the appropriate measure of fertility to use in such an inquiry would be that displayed in figure 3. However, it is apparent that the variations to be explained are quite small; only a major war can make these short-term deviations in period fertility exceed more than a few per cent per annum.

The index plotted in figure 3 is a pure tempo phenomenon. It is natural for us to think of the effects of circumstances of a particular year as moving the quantum of fertility up or down, yet when

we try to explain such movements, we employ terms like postponement and preponement. These refer to the occurrence of births to
the relevant cohorts at a later or earlier time than they would otherwise have been expected to occur, without consequence for the
quantum of cohort fertility. In brief, they are short-run variations
in cohort tempo. They may lead eventually to a shortfall or longfall
in the quantum of cohort fertility, but that is a substantive question
(discussed in the section on 'alternative models') and a departure
from the sense of postponement and preponement themselves.

In this section, we have shown that the period total fertility rate
reflects long-term movements of cohort quantum and tempo, and
also a short-term oscillation which is a manifestation of cohort
tempo variations, particularly in response to wars. With the data at
hand, little more can be said about the last source of change. The
remainder of the paper deals with the components of long-term
variations in cohort quantum and tempo.

Components of the Quantum of Cohort Fertility

We now shift the mode of temporal aggregation and the time
series representation from periods to cohorts. The basic curves we
are attempting to explain are those shown in figure 4. (The data for
$G(T)$ are shown in table 3, and for $M(T)$ in table 4.) The movements
of $G(T)$ are those manifested in the quantum component of period
fertility ($G(t)$ in figure 2) smoothed in moving average fashion, and
the movements of the complement of the time-derivative of $M(T)$
are those manifested in the long-term tempo component of period
fertility ($d(t)$ in figure 2, bereft of its short-term deviations). The
series of cohorts with which we are working proceed from c.1891 to
c.1950. To orient oneself to the more familiar time series of calendar years, one can think of each cohort as located approximately at
the time corresponding to its mean age of fertility—the values of
which range from 24 to 28. Thus the series displayed here correspond approximately in time span with the earlier figures.

Discussion of the movements of $G(T)$ and $M(T)$ is deferred until
the section on 'alternative models'. Our present purpose is to use
the available data to decompose movements of $G(T)$ (see Appendix
3). The first possibility that would occur to one is the completed
parity distribution, $P(y)$. The cohort total fertility rate has the
attractive feature of being the mean of that distribution, since it is

the mean number of births per woman. The completed parity distribution may be of great interest in analysis of the consequences of
the reproductive process, but it is doubtful whether it is in a useful
form to explain that process. Admittedly such a calculation would
be appropriate for a model in which the eventual parity of a woman
was a lifetime target toward which she moved inexorably from
menarche onward. If such a model were plausible, the parity distribution, as an indication of the relative attractiveness of different
targets, would be the calculation of choice. It is apparent, however,
that such a conceptualization is far from the mark in studying a
stochastic and error-ridden process. The woman achieves her final
parity in a series of discrete problematic steps (barring the empirically trivial exception of multiple births). The probability of each
step depends on considerations of the couple's reproductive decision (positive or negative, if any) and of the ability of the couple to
fulfil a positive decision (a question of fecundability) or a negative
decision (a question of the efficacy of fertility regulation in relation
to fecundability).

Accordingly, a more appropriate orientation, to set the stage for

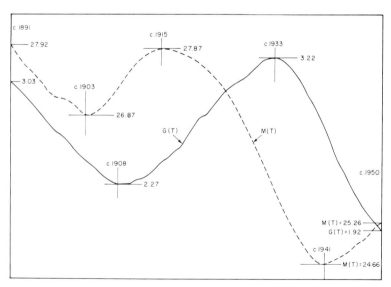

Figure 4.   Cohort Quantum and Tempo. Cohort Total Fertility Rate,
$G(T)$; Cohort Mean Age of Fertility $M(T)$; USA, cc.1891–1950.

Table 3.   Components of the quantum of cohort fertility, cc. 1891–1950, US.

T	G(T)	L(T)	H(T)	T	G(T)	L(T)	H(T)
1891	3·0322	0·8014	0·7120	1921	2·7652	0·8548	0·6175
1892	2·9833	0·8011	0·7059	1922	2·7940	0·8582	0·6181
1893	2·9364	0·7993	0·7010	1923	2·8467	0·8646	0·6228
1894	2·8088	0·7969	0·6952	1924	2·9131	0·8725	0·6269
1895	2·8303	0·7945	0·6899	1925	2·9657	0·8772	0·6315
1896	2·7729	0·7906	0·6847	1926	3·0065	0·8801	0·6357
1897	2·7176	0·7870	0·6792	1927	3·0413	0·8820	0·6397
1898	2·6719	0·7832	0·6751	1928	3·0693	0·8836	0·6428
1899	2·6353	0·7790	0·6730	1929	3·1226	0·8888	0·6463
1900	2·5826	0·7720	0·6708	1930	3·1565	0·8927	0·6479
1901	2·5253	0·7678	0·6646	1931	3·2004	0·8993	0·6485
1902	2·4768	0·7654	0·6576	1932	3·2149	0·9034	0·6469
1903	2·4419	0·7650	0·6510	1933	3·2206	0·9066	0·6448
1904	2·4050	0·7617	0·6469	1934	3·2078	0·9087	0·6408
1905	2·3585	0·7564	0·6428	1935	3·1667	0·9074	0·6355
1906	2·3179	0·7530	0·6376	1936	3·1083	0·9053	0·6279
1907	2·2945	0·7533	0·6317	1937	3·0378	0·9024	0·6186
1908	2·2703	0·7531	0·6261	1938	2·9541	0·8987	0·6069
1909	2·2728	0·7566	0·6224	1939	2·8781	0·8962	0·5946
1910	2·2742	0·7593	0·6193	1940	2·7824	0·8915	0·5795
1911	2·2956	0·7656	0·6168	1941	2·6762	0·8849	0·5628
1912	2·3119	0·7719	0·6130	1942	2·5644	0·8782	0·5426
1913	2·3428	0·7809	0·6096	1943	2·4521	0·8689	0·5230
1914	2·3877	0·7914	0·6076	1944	2·3554	0·8605	0·5046
1915	2·4338	0·8014	0·6068	1945	2·2593	0·8502	0·4870
1916	2·4672	0·8074	0·6072	1946	2·1839	0·8439	0·4684
1917	2·5121	0·8157	0·6077	1947	2·1013	0·8337	0·4515
1918	2·5502	0·8223	0·6086	1948	2·0395	0·8271	0·4356
1919	2·6379	0·8365	0·6114	1949	1·9771	0·8160	0·4264
1920	2·7023	0·8461	0·6142	1950	1·9202	0·8066	0·4158

$G(T)$ = Cohort total fertility rate.
$L(T)$ = Low-parity component.
$H(T)$ = High-parity component.
$G(T) = L(T) + (L^2(T)/(1 - H(T)))$.

intensive probing in those directions with other research instruments, would be a direct measure of the probability of advancing from each parity to the next (accompanied by a measure of the length of time involved in the passage from each parity to the next, the topic of the following section). This was the thinking behind our devising, in the late 1940s, the parity progression ratio, the

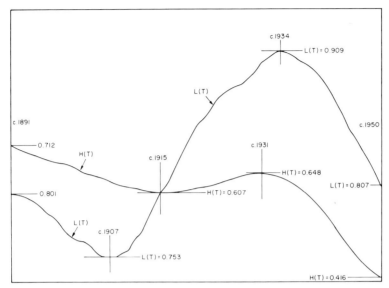

Figure 5. Components of Quantum of Cohort Fertility. Low-parity
Component, $L(T)$; High-parity Component, $H(T)$;
$$G(T) = L(T) + L^2(T)/(1 - H(T))$$
(Components scaled independently; scale of $L(T)$ three times scale of
$H(T)$) USA, cc.1891–1950.

probability that a woman with at least y births would have at least
$y + 1$ births eventually. Independently, Louis Henry came to the
same conclusion; his term for the measure was 'probabilité
d'aggrandissement'. He has developed powerful applications of the
measure, particularly with respect to his concept of 'natural
fertility'.

The algebra of parity progression ratios is discussed in Appendix
3. We have routinely produced parity progression ratios for the
successive parities, for our cohort series. Rather than run the risk
of being overwhelmed by the embarrassment of empirical riches
this yields, we have attempted to capture the principal features of
the parity components of total fertility by focusing on an average
progression ratio for parities zero and one (labelled L, for low-
parity), and an average progression ratio for all higher parities
(labelled H). These are shown in figure 5 (and table 3).

Both theoretical and empirical justification can be provided for
this particular dichotomization. In our judgement, social norms in

Table 4. Components of the tempo of cohort
fertility, cc.1891–1950, US.

T	$M(T)$	$M(1, T)$	$I(T)$	$K(T)$
1891	27·9222	23·3855	2·4316	1·8657
1892	27·7840	23·3570	2·4591	1·8002
1893	27·6414	23·3162	2·4794	1·7444
1894	27·5366	23·2756	2·5195	1·6912
1895	27·4391	23·2478	2·5488	1·6444
1896	27·3252	23·2072	2·5842	1·5935
1897	27·2195	23·1590	2·6254	1·5466
1898	27·1425	23·1272	2·6462	1·5173
1899	27·1316	23·1452	2·6598	1·4987
1900	27·0923	23·1383	2·6825	1·4739
1901	27·0162	23·1369	2·7330	1·4194
1902	26·9158	23·1122	2·7882	1·3641
1903	26·8684	23·1263	2·8066	1·3333
1904	26·9034	23·1992	2·8642	1·2932
1905	26·9723	23·3052	2·8947	1·2668
1906	27·0547	23·4162	2·9399	1·2376
1907	27·1699	23·5710	2·9726	1·2106
1908	27·2781	23·7132	3·0047	1·1864
1909	27·4263	23·8787	3·0167	1·1759
1910	27·5625	24·0200	3·0375	1·1663
1911	27·6562	24·1076	3·0598	1·1597
1912	27·7374	24·1793	3·0977	1·1486
1913	27·8000	24·2333	3·1318	1·1388
1914	27·8565	24·2687	3·1477	1·1398
1915	27·8738	24·2535	3·1603	1·1455
1916	27·8627	24·2114	3·1597	1·1555
1917	27·8524	24·1614	3·1592	1·1683
1918	27·8024	24·0751	3·1610	1·1791
1919	27·7714	23·9707	3·1771	1·1962
1920	27·7088	23·8452	3·1882	1·2118
1921	27·6365	23·7252	3·1741	1·2322
1922	27·5763	23·6267	3·1670	1·2471
1923	27·4914	23·5159	3·1376	1·2670
1924	27·3855	23·3762	3·0960	1·2949
1925	27·2581	23·2359	3·0372	1·3243
1926	27·1086	23·0986	2·9633	1·3532
1927	26·9332	22·9592	2·8856	1·3771
1928	26·7433	22·8199	2·8062	1·3981
1929	26·5619	22·6876	2·7240	1·4222
1930	26·3620	22·5688	2·6474	1·4328
1931	26·1493	22·4441	2·5806	1·4357
1932	25·9396	22·3310	2·5313	1·4255
1933	25·7247	22·2123	2·4925	1·4091

Table 4.   (continued)

T	M(T)	M(1,T)	I(T)	K(T)
1934	25·5272	22·1154	2·4627	1·3853
1935	25·3435	22·0412	2·4422	1·3521
1936	25·1673	21·9848	2·4318	1·3087
1937	25·0048	21·9492	2·4297	1·2576
1938	24·8595	21·9269	2·4468	1·1985
1939	24·7451	21·9183	2·4644	1·1470
1940	24·6665	21·9499	2·5199	1·0789
1941	24·6553	22·0405	2·5837	1·0120
1942	24·6810	22·1603	2·6758	0·9420
1943	24·7242	22·2769	2·7893	0·8773
1944	24·7679	22·3715	2·9105	0·8233
1945	24·8250	22·4854	3·0243	0·7736
1946	24·9159	22·5912	3·1990	0·7266
1947	24·9906	22·6679	3·3924	0·6841
1948	25·0863	22·7935	3·5589	0·6442
1949	25·1783	22·9236	3·6452	0·6185
1950	25·2566	23·0439	3·7350	0·5924

$M(T)$ = Mean age of cohort fertility.
$M(1, T)$ = Mean age of cohort first order fertility.
$I(T)$ = Mean interbirth interval.
$K(T)$ = Interval scale factor.

the United States, at least until very recently, pressed people into a preference for marriage over non-marriage, parenthood over non-parenthood, and at least two children rather than an only child— with the proviso that one should be able to fulfil one's parental obligations. Beyond the second child, the progression is primarily a matter of individual preference (although friends, neighbours and relatives may begin to look askance should the number exceed four or five).

To provide an empirical support for the division, we calculated the median difference between progression ratios for successive parities, over the sixty cohorts. The difference was 0·05 between parities zero and one, 0·16 between parities one and two, 0·05 between parities two and three, and 0·00 between parities three and (four or more). This speaks strongly for a division between parities one and two, i.e. between L and H. Furthermore, each of the first four parities has a time series of progression ratios with a pronounced peak after an early decline. We have compared the size of that peak with the initial value (for c.1891) with the following results: + 15% for parity zero, + 12% for parity one, − 1% for parity two, and − 11% for parity three. Once again, the two lower parities are distinguished from the others. Likewise we compared the final value (for c.1950) with that of the peak, and found that the first two parities showed declines of 10% and 14%, whereas the last two parities showed declines of 38% and 44%. It is most encouraging to find such strong empirical support for a position espoused on theoretical grounds. The implicit argument is that one should look within the realm of normative pressures in relation to the socio-economic context for explanation of variations in L, but within the realm of discretionary reproduction for explanation of variations in H (although the latter will be the repository of indiscreet reproduction as well).

The plotting of the graphs of L and H in figure 5 uses a scale for L which is three times the scale of H, as a rough-and-ready allowance for the relative importance of each in the constitution of G. The dominant feature of the experience is a large fluctuation in L, and no more than a slight interruption in the decline in H. The validity of the latter characterization would be much more apparent if we had more temporal perspective concerning cohorts before c.1891. We have quantum estimates for cohorts back to c.1867, for which the value of L was 4% higher than that for c.1891, while the value of H was 10% higher than that for c.1891. It seems plausible that H has been declining steadily since the beginning of the nineteenth century (when it was probably in the neighbourhood of 0·9) whereas the range of variation of L is probably encompassed by the extremes of figure 5.

While this is not the place for an analysis of such movements, it may be worth observing in passing that the recent decline in H is less surprising in perspective than the brief and modest departure from a downward trend. The fluctuation in L is more difficult to characterize. On the one hand, the peak for c.1934 may have been an aberration and the current decline a return to a more 'normal' level. On the other hand, given the strength of reproductive norms pressing toward at least two children if they could be afforded, one may say that the peak for c.1934 represented a culmination of that pronatalist pressure, in a favourable socio-economic climate. The issue would then become whether the recent decline is a temporary reaction to cloudy conditions (an implausible proposition in light of the high level of real per capita income) or a signal of something new on the normative horizon. Our strong belief is that the latter is the case—that motherhood itself is becoming a matter of preference.

For the recent cohorts, the values are estimates based on an assumption. To test the robustness of those estimates in the face of alternative assumptions, we projected fertility beyond 1976·0 with rates 20% higher than those of 1975. The outcome would have been a level of G which was 7% higher than that projected for c.1950, decomposed into a 3% higher level for L, and a 5% higher level for H. Otherwise said, the values we now have for c.1948 would have applied rather to c.1950. Nothing of substance would need to be changed in our account by such a substitution.

Components of the tempo of cohort fertility

The only information in the cohort fertility tables bearing on the tempo of fertility is the time-distribution of fertility for each birth order. One naturally thinks first, on a question of the time pattern of reproduction, of nuptiality data, specifically the age at first marriage. While there are quite useful series from which one can develop cohort nuptiality estimates for the United States, they pose the classic difficulty of merging series from different sources, when the purpose is to calculate differences. Moreover, there has clearly occurred in the recent past an attenuation of the link between marriage and exposure to risk of fertility. With these two considerations in mind, we have decided to focus on the age at entry into parenthood rather than the age at first marriage, as a beginning for the tempo calculations.

The ideal kind of information one would like to use, subsequent to entry into parenthood, would be the length of interval from each birth to the next. That would require fertility rates specific not only for age and parity, but also for interval since last birth. For most states, data are now being published which give the numerators for such rates, but the appropriate denominators do not yet exist. Also, for a few recent groups of cohorts, the 1970 Census contained the requisite information (used in Appendix 4). But there is literally no way of exploiting for interval length the tempting long series of

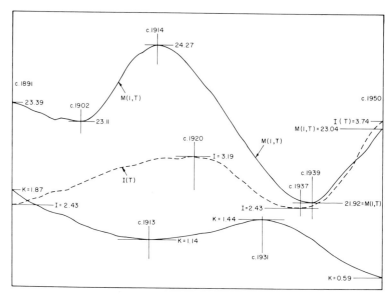

Figure 6.   Components of Tempo of Cohort Fertility. Mean Age at First Birth, $M(1, T)$; Mean Interbirth Interval, $I(T)$; Interval Scale Factor, $K(T)$; Mean Age of Cohort Fertility $= M(1, T) + K(T)*I(T)$ (Components scaled independently) USA, cc.1891–1950.

cohort fertility calculations without an assumption. The procedure followed is explained in Appendix 4.

The summary of cohort variations in the tempo of reproduction is captured in the equation $M = M(1) + K*I$, that is, the mean age of cohort fertility (shown in figure 4) is the sum of the mean age of first order fertility and a particular number (K) of intervals of mean length I. These components are shown in figure 6 (and table 4). The dominant variable within this system is clearly $M(1)$. Although the movements of I have not been insubstantial, they have been counterbalanced by movements of the scale factor K, giving an approximately constant product $K*I$ throughout. This point is returned to in the final section. One point of detail about interval length I is that low-order intervals tend to be somewhat longer than high-order intervals. With an increase in the representation of low-order intervals (a decline in K), there is a tendency for I to lengthen.

In the discussion of the age distribution component of the crude birth rate, $c(t)$, in the first section of this paper, the question was raised of an intelligible explanation for the compensatory movements of $c(t)$ and $F(t)$. In our judgment, the most likely explanation is that the size of one's cohort (captured by the value $c(t)$) is most likely to affect one's time of entry into parenthood. A comparison of the graph of $c(t)$ from figure 1, and of $M(1, T)$ from figure 6, indicates a close correspondence between these. The reason for this judgment is that the disadvantage of belonging to a large cohort, and conversely the advantage of belonging to a small cohort, is a question of how difficult or easy one's entry into adult life is as a consequence, and that would be registered most clearly in the age at entry into parenthood. Since such modifications of the tempo of cohort childbearing are strongly influential on the quantum of period fertility, it would not be surprising if correlations would also be observed with such quantum indices, but it is our opinion that they are reflections of the underlying link between cohort size and age at beginning of reproduction.

In the presentation in figure 6, and in table 4, K is a residual scale factor calculated by taking the ratio $[M - M(1)]/I$. In order to get an intuitive feeling for this measure, we determined for a simple model that K is approximately equal to $(\phi - 1)*G/(G + 1)$, where ϕ is the mean order of birth (see Appendix 4). Now the mean order of birth reflects not only the mean parity but also the variance of the parity distribution. Specifically, $\phi = [G(1 + c^2) + 1]/2$, where c is the coefficient of variation of the parity distribution. The value c changed little from the initial value to the trough of fertility (c.1908), and then declined, by about one-third, to the time of the peak (c.1933), since when it has changed little. This shift from heterogeneity to homogeneity of the parity distribution in the United States has played a small but interesting role in the history of period fertility. Had the coefficient of variation of the parity distribution remained fixed throughout the span of sixty cohorts, the period total fertility rate would have declined by 3% more than it did from the beginning to the trough, it would have risen by 8% more than it did from the trough to the peak, and it would have declined by 7% more from the peak to the end. In other words, the shift toward greater parity homogeneity helped to dampen the swings in period fertility throughout the past sixty years.

We note the consequences for our tempo measures of departures from the projection assumption. Had we projected the fertility level at 20% above that chosen, the value of M would have been 1·5% higher than that reported, the value of $M(1)$ would have been 0·7% higher, the value of I 1·% higher, and the value of K 8·7% higher. As was the case with the quantum parameters, the result would essentially have been to replace the values reported for c. 1950 by the values reported for c.1948. No substantive consequence emerges from invalidity of the projection assumption.

Allocation of responsibility for movements of the period total fertility rate

As a way of summarizing the three preceding sections, and of assessing the relative magnitudes of influence of each of the identified components of fertility change, we have developed a procedure for combining the results of our various measurements (see Appendix 5). In the second section, we decomposed the period total fertility rate into three parts: (1) a measure of long-term variations in the quantum of fertility, explained as a moving average of the cohort total fertility rate; (2) a measure of long-term distributional distortion, closely captured by the complement of the time-derivative of the cohort mean age of fertility; (3) a residual which we called the short-term period effect, excluded from present consideration. The initial step in our procedure is to identify the proportions of change associated with the first measure (dependent on movements of the quantum of cohort fertility) and with the second measure (dependent on movements of the tempo of cohort fertility). The former in turn can be subdivided, following the account in the third section, into a low-parity and a high-parity component, again expressed as complementary proportions of the total; the latter in turn can be subdivided, following the account in the fourth section, into components associated with the mean age at first birth, the interbirth interval, and the interval scale factor. Since the last of these is a reflection of changes in the quantum of cohort fertility, we have re-allocated its contribution to the quantum side of the ledger; it represents the indirect effect on tempo of quantum changes.

The results of this exercise have been produced for the time series of fertility, subdivided into three episodes. The period total fertility rate moved downward from the beginning of the series to a trough,

Table 5. Proportion of change in long-term period total fertility rate
associated with change in five components of cohort fertility.

	From beginning to trough	From trough to peak	From peak to end
Quantum effect	0·696	0·424	0·448
Low-parity	0·195	0·367	0·218
High-parity	0·337	0·042	0·363
Scale effect on tempo	0·164	0·015	0·134
Tempo effect	0·304	0·576	0·552
Age at 1st birth	0·335	0·443	0·309
Interbirth interval	0·051	0·133	0·243

then rose to a peak, and finally declined to its current value. The same kind of description can be applied to the cohort total fertility rate displayed in figure 4. Because of the critical role played by movements of the cohort parameters, the trough and peak were identified for them, at c.1908 and c.1933 respectively. Given the requirement of time-derivatives of some of the cohort parameters, for which purpose we chose to employ a seven-term moving quadratic fit, the cohort series was truncated by three terms at either end; accordingly the beginning cohort is c.1894 and the end cohort is c.1947. The comparable periods were selected on the basis of the value of the mean cohort in each period (the cohort closest to the period mean age of fertility); the corresponding years for the beginning, trough, peak, and end are 1922, 1936, 1957, and 1972 respectively. It so happens that 1936 and 1957 were, in fact, the trough and peak of the period series.

The results of this exercise are shown in table 5. The first result of significance is the comparative relevance of quantum and tempo changes on the period total fertility rate. While movements of the quantum of cohort fertility provided 70% of the explanation in the first episode, movements of the tempo of cohort fertility have been dominant since then. Said otherwise, most of the baby boom would have occurred without any change whatsoever in the numbers of births per woman, and most of the decline since the baby boom as well. In terms of the subdivisions of the quantum effect, the high-parity component was the most influential in the first and last episodes, but played an insignificant role in the baby boom. Consider what this implies for an evaluation of our research efforts over the past several decades. The series of national fertility surveys every five years since 1955 in the United States was designed to serve many purposes, but central among them was explanation of the temporal variations in fertility during the episode of the baby boom and the most recent episode of decline. In attempting to fulfil that assignment, we followed the overwhelming consensus of demographic opinion in devoting the bulk of our attention to the numbers of children born to women, and especially the numbers of unwanted children. It is evident from table 5 that the numbers of children born were of less importance than their time pattern of birth, and more particularly that the numbers of unwanted children —a subset of the high-parity component—played scarcely any role in variations in period fertility during the baby boom episode.

An interesting role has been played, within the quantum sector, by the scale factor (the indirect effect on the tempo of fertility of changes in the parity mean and variance). Its influence was strong and positive in the initial episode, negligible in the baby boom (because of the shrinkage of parity variance during that time) and strong and negative during the last episode—as the reduction of high-parity fertility worked to counterbalance the rise in the mean age of fertility.

The principal driving force behind movements of period fertility since the trough has been changes in the tempo of cohort fertility. Of the two components of those changes, the dominant element has been changes in the age at first birth, although a growing role has been played by the length of the interbirth interval. We are unaware of important contributions to the explanation of the age at entry into parenthood; certainly, little attention has been paid to it in our series of fertility surveys. Indeed, we doubt that we have a clear sense of the appropriate way to approach the question. For example, we have devoted considerable attention to the question of the number of births each woman reports that she intends to have, with not a little success, but our efforts to get usable statements concerning the intended time pattern of fertility have gone for naught (Westoff & Ryder, 1977).

On the evidence presented, it would seem sensible to assign a high priority to research on the determinants of the tempo of cohort fertility and of the progression ratios for parities zero and one. Now it may be objected that, although we have come to this conclusion on the basis of examination of a time series covering sixty annual birth cohorts, the experience is in fact dominated by a single long wave in the absence of a significant trend in the quantum of cohort fertility. Admitting that this restricts the generality of the findings, our response would be that the future, in low-fertility countries, is more likely to be characterized by further such long waves about a lower asymptote than by a trend in the quantum of fertility (up or down) without such waves. As for high-fertility countries, the question is moot in the absence of reliable and detailed data over time, but it would not seem implausible, in principle, that the anticipated transformation of their fertility will also have a substantial tempo component, and significant changes in the low parities.

Alternative models of fertility measurement

In the preceding account, we have presented a measurement system based implicitly on two premises: first, that the cohort is the appropriate focus for causal analysis and what is observed in a period is a distorted manifestation of the underlying cohort behaviour, and second, that it is worthwhile from an analytic standpoint to distinguish clearly between the quantum and tempo aspects of reproduction. Our final task is to assess the conceptual justification for this approach.

A convenient beginning for the account is consideration of the movements, in figure 4, of G and M, i.e. the cohort total fertility rate and mean age of fertility. Although G and M generally move inversely to one another, there are three episodes during which this is not so. Over the span covering cc.1891–1903, G and M were both declining. The explanation for this departure from an inverse relationship is that both quantum and tempo may be expected to decline in an era in which the reductions of fertility are disproportionately at the higher orders of birth (and thus in the older ages). Otherwise stated, this is a consequence of change in the scale factor, K, rather than a genuine contradiction of the principle that quantum and tempo move inversely.

The other two episodes are triggered by the inception of the rise in fertility, from c.1908, and by the inception of the fall in fertility, from c.1933 (each continuing for seven or eight cohorts). These episodes of direct relationship between quantum and tempo movements are the consequence of a kind of period effect not previously noted. If all cohorts experience a rise in fertility, beginning in the same period, the consequence is a rise in the mean age of fertility for all cohorts which at that time are beyond their mean age of fertility. Likewise, if all cohorts experience a decline in fertility, beginning in the same period, the consequence is a decline in the mean age of fertility for all cohorts which at that time are beyond the mean age of fertility.

The style of presentation in the preceding sections has emphasized the consequences for period quantum of changes in cohort tempo; what we have just observed is the consequences for cohort tempo of changes in period quantum. There are alternative models of the reproductive process, depending on whether the period or the cohort is considered to be the dominant vector of influence. In one model, the cohorts pass through a sequence of periods, responding in much the same way (albeit on an age-differentiated basis) to the succession of favourable or unfavourable conditions. In this model, the cohort quantum and tempo parameters are like moving averages of response to the sequence of period-specific conditions. In the other model, implicitly advocated in this paper, the cohort follows a largely predetermined trajectory toward a particular target with respect to quantum and tempo, modified in detail in response to the alternation of favourable and unfavourable periods. In this latter model, the record of a period is a distorted depiction of underlying intercohort change, because the person examining the statistics for successive periods is looking at cohort change through a prism. It would be difficult to deny the merits of either alternative at face value.

From a statistical standpoint, modes of temporal aggregation are on equal footing. The approach we have followed above to the summarization of a surface of fertility rates specific for (period or cohort) time and age could have been conducted without modification in the opposite direction. That is to say, the distributional distortion could have been calculated from the sum of period proportions in successive cohorts, and related in the same manner to the period mean age of fertility; the subsequent decomposition of quantum and tempo parameters could have been conducted on period rather than cohort functions. In other words, this is another example of the failure of the stance that one should let the facts speak for themselves. Measures reflect models, and models reflect theoretical choices made on substantive grounds not in evidence in the data considered here.

The second premise of the approach adopted in this paper is that quantum and tempo are independent facets of cohort reproductive behaviour. To examine this question, we proceed from the previous observation that it is generally the case that the cohort total fertility rate and the cohort mean age of fertility move in opposite directions. The point may be observed more clearly in figure 6. Here we have a pure tempo measure (I), and a measure of quantum, the scale factor (K). They evidently move inversely to one another, with little exception. This is not a surprising finding. It has long been observed, from cross-sectional comparisons, that completed parity tends to vary inversely with the age at first marriage, and that interval length tends to vary inversely with completed parity. These relationships are complementary to the diachronic observations reported previously in this paper.

We may identify important sources of the inverse relationship between quantum and tempo for three contexts of fertility regulation. Consider first a population, or the women in a particular parity, in which there is no planning of fertility. For this situation, the quantum and tempo parameters are two facets of a single underlying probability distribution of fecundability. Lower fecundability, whatever the source, would be expected to yield a larger proportion with zero fecundability (a lower parity progression ratio) and a longer waiting time for those with non-zero fecundability. In this situation, quantum and tempo are two faces of the same coin.

The context of completely and successfully planned reproduction is somewhat more complex. We may think of two distinct decisions to be made by couples—whether to have another birth and, if so, after how long a time. If there were a correlation between the outcome of these two decisions, it would arise from substantive roots. It is an empirical question whether a woman who wants more babies also wants to have babies sooner, and at shorter intervals, although it is not implausible that a strong normative pressure toward parenthood would manifest itself in both the quantum and tempo directions.

Consider, also, the situation with respect to short-term variations in a context of perfect planning. We have previously described postponement and preponement as pure cohort tempo concepts. More realistically, the deferral of a birth from age x to some future age, say $x + dx$, leaves open the question whether, by the time age $x + dx$ is reached, the postponed birth will in fact occur, since some may change their intention. The preponement of a birth from x to $x - dx$, on the other hand, leaves open the option of whether to have yet another birth, once x is reached. As an aside, there is an upward bias to fertility which is related to irreversibility. The baby born earlier than usual, in response to temporarily favourable conditions, has already occurred, and nothing can be done about it if conditions subsequently become unfavourable. On the other hand, the baby not born earlier, in response to temporarily unfavourable conditions, may or may not occur subsequently if conditions become favourable.

The most apt illustration of the interpenetration of tempo and quantum considerations in a perfectly planned context comes from consideration of the reproductive decision itself. Implicit in the foregoing account is the idea of a couple first fixing on a quantum target and then determining a tempo target. A more realistic situation in the short run, and perhaps in the long run as well, would be one in which the couple face the question each month as to whether they want to conceive in that month. Whether the answer is affirmative or negative, the decision cannot be construed as either quantum or tempo in type, since it is both.

The general point is that tempo decisions, in a perfectly planned situation, may have quantum consequences, or may be indistinguishable from quantum decisions. One of the dramatic fertility movements of the past thirty years was the concomitant decline and then rise in tempo components (figure 6), and the rise and then decline in quantum components. Our proposal is that the movements of tempo were not irrelevant to the movements of quantum, and that the two are to some degree alternative manifestations of the same underlying behaviour.

The most likely context of fertility regulation is a state of imperfect planning. A higher risk of failure is translated on the one hand into a higher parity progression ratio and on the other into a shorter interbirth interval; the converse is true for a lower risk of failure. Moreover, an earlier beginning to fertility implies, for any particular number of children intended, a lower age at time of the last intended child, and thus an earlier exposure to risk of unintended children. In other words, a lower tempo becomes translated into a higher quantum.

Our conclusion is that we cannot, in principle, make a statistical separation of the tempo and quantum facets of fertility. Our choice among alternative representations depends very much on what we may know about the distribution of the reproducing population by intention, and by the extent and effectiveness of fertility regulation. It would follow, then, that the framework of vital statistics, as exploited here, is insufficient to enable one to come to decisions about appropriate measurement procedures, in the absence of behavioural surveys designed to explore the structure of intentions and the use of means to fulfil those intentions. And even with such data, we are left with the conceptual conundrum of identifying the forces primarily responsible for the movements we are attempting to measure, and therefore of identifying which are the appropriate measures to use. The message with respect to the quantum and tempo dimensions is, in the end, the same as the message with respect to the cohort and period modes of temporal orientation: we cannot design good measures without good theory.

Acknowledgement

This work was supported by a contract with the Center for Population Research, National Institute of Child Health and Human Development.

Appendix 1. The birth rate and the age distribution factor

The crude birth rate, $b(t) = 1000*B(t)/Y(t)$, where $B(t)$ are births in year t, and $Y(t)$ are person-years for the total population in that year.

The cohort fertility tables provide age-specific birth rates for ages 14–19 inclusive, for years 1917–75 inclusive.

The age-specific birth rate, $f(x, t) = B(x, t)/Y'(x, t)$, where $B(x, t)$ are births in year t to women of age x at time of birth, and $Y'(x,t)$ are the person-years spent by women in age x in year t.

The period total fertility rate, $F(t) = \Sigma f(x, t)$. (All sums in these appendices, unless specifically noted otherwise, are over ages $x = 14, 49$.)

Then the crude birth rate may be expressed as $b(t) = 1000*\Sigma\ c(x, t)*f(x, t)$ where $c(x, t) = Y'(x, t)/Y(t)$.

The age distribution factor, $c(t) = b(t)/F(t) = 1000*\Sigma p(x, t)*c(x, t)$ where $p(x, t) = f(x, t)/F(t)$. One can think of $c(t)$ as an average value for $c(x, t)$, centred on some age A, presumably close in value to the mean age of period fertility $A(t) = \Sigma x*p(x, t)$.

In a closed population, $c(A, t) = Y'(A, t)/Y(t)$
$$= h*S(A)*B(t - A)/Y(t)$$
$$= h*S(A)*(B(t - A)/Y(t - A))$$
$$* (Y(t - A)/Y(t))$$
$$= h*S(A)*b(t - A)*\exp(-rA)$$

where h is the proportion of births female, essentially a constant, $S(A)$ is the proportion of female babies surviving from $t - A$ to t and r is the growth rate between $t - A$ and t. For the values of changes in these components, cited in the text, we set $A = 25$.

Appendix 2. Distributional distortion

(a)   Estimates of cohort fertility

With the data from the cohort fertility tables for ages 14–49, for years 1917–75, one can derive, without estimation, complete reproductive histories from the cohort at the youngest age in the earliest year (c.1903 was age 14 in 1917) to the cohort at the oldest age in the latest year (c.1926 was age 49 in 1975). To develop a longer series, we both retrojected and projected the data. Retrojection is a simple task because, in addition to the indicated data, cumulated total fertility rates are provided for all cohorts in the reproductive age span in 1917 (cumulated to the beginning of 1917). Thus the quantum component for these cohorts need not be estimated, but only the time distribution of that part of fertility which occurred prior to 1917. The method used, for the cohorts back to c.1891, was to assume that the distribution of fertility over the ages from 14 through the age in 1916, for each cohort, was the same as the distribution of fertility over the same age span in 1917.

Projection beyond c.1926 was a much more challenging assignment. We decided to project the series as far as c.1950, which was 26·0 at the end of the data set. Projection requires estimation of both tempo and quantum components. The projection is less bold than would seem at first glance, because of the current tendency to terminate childbearing at a rather early age.

Deliberately, one assumption was employed in the projection— that the age–parity-specific fertility rates for 1975 remain fixed throughout the remaining reproductive lifetimes of the cohorts to be projected. The form of the rate requires some explanation.

The cohort fertility tables for the United States consist of alternative representations of a basic data set, $g(x, y, T) = B(x, y, T)/Y'(x, T)$, i.e. the ratio of (births of order y which occur in age x to women born in year T) to the (sum of person-years spent in age x by women born in year T). The registration data actually come in the form $B(x, y, t)$, where t is the calendar year of occurrence, and x is the age at last birthday. The births are thus an approximation of births occurring to women born within six months on either side of exact time $T = t - x$, a 'fiscal' birth cohort with time of birth centred on the beginning of year T. In actuality, the appropriate births would be those occurring within a laterally symmetric triangle of age and time, with a base which is two years rather than one in length.

$g(x, y, T) = f(x, y, T)$, where $T = t - x$. This is an age-specific fertility rate for a female birth cohort, with the numerator restricted to births of a particular order y. It is convenient for subsequent development to define a cumulative rate up to exact age x.

$$G(X, y, T) = \sum_{i = 14}^{x - 1} g(i, y, T)$$

Henceforth we will suppress the cohort designation T. These cumulative rates permit a specification of the parity distribution of women at each exact age, since the proportion of women in parity y at exact age x consist of those who have had a yth birth by age X, but have not (yet) had a $y + 1$th birth.

$P(X, y) = G(X, y)$ for $y = 0,6$, where $G(X,0) = 1$.

$P(X, 7+) = G(7)$.

This provides the denominator for a measure published in the cohort fertility tables, and called there an age–parity–specific birth probability—defined as follows:

$u(x, y) = g(x, y + 1)/P(X, y)$ for $y = 0, 6$

$u(x, 7+) = g(x, 8+)/P(X, 7+)$.

This is the most detailed piece of information available for fertility analysis in these tables (except for the dichotomization of all women into 'whites' and 'all others', not considered here). On two grounds, we have chosen to make an alternative calculation. In the first place, the measure $u(x, y)$ is ill-named, since it is not a probability. There is no well-defined set of women who, at the beginning of an age, can be identified as those exposed to the risk of a $y + 1$th birth in that age, since there are additions to their numbers throughout the age (by the occurrence of further yth births to the cohort). In such a situation (of increment as well as decrement), the appropriate measure is a central rate of the familiar occurrence/exposure variety. In the second place, exposure to risk of a $y + 1$th birth ordinarily begins no sooner than a year (more or less) after entry into parity y—aside from the empirically trivial circumstance of multiple births. Since the principal usefulness of measures like these is to provide a precise indication of short-term variations in fertility, the advantage of this consideration is obvious.

Accordingly we recommend the following central age–parity–specific fertility rate:

$v(x, y) = 2*g(x, y + 1)/(G(X - 1, y) + G(X,y)-G(X,y + 1)-$
    $G(X + 1, y + 1))$ for $y = 0, 6$
$v(x,7+) = 2*g(x, 8+)/(G(X - 1, 7) + G(X, 7))$.

For the purpose of projection with such measures, one requires a recursion form. Although probabilities are ordinarily used for this purpose, the values $v(x, y)$ can be readily adapted to the task. Define $w(x, y) = (2 - v(x, y))/(2 + v(x, y))$

Then $G(X + 1, y + 1) = (w(x, y)*G(X, y + 1)) + ((1 - w(x, y))*(G(X - 1, y) + G(X, y))/2)$ for $y = 0, 6$
$G(X + 1, 8+) = v(x, 7+)*(G(X -1, 7) + G(X, 7))/2$.

(b) Distributional distortion measures
$p(x, T = t -x) = f(x, t)/G(T = t - x)$
$d(t) = \Sigma p(x, T)$
$G(t) \quad F(t)/d(t)$
    $= F(t)/\Sigma (f(x, t)/G(T))$
    $= 1/\Sigma((f(x, t)/F(t))*(1/G(T)))$
    $= 1/\Sigma(p(x, t)/G(T))$
    = the weighted harmonic mean of the total fertility rates

of those cohorts bearing children in year t, where the weights are the proportions of the period total fertility rate contributed by each cohort.

The harmonic mean is a little smaller than the arithmetic mean, the amount of the difference depending largely on the magnitude of the coefficient of variation. With small deviations relative to the mean, it is approximately the case that the harmonic mean is equal to the product of the arithmetic mean and the complement of the square of the coefficient of variation. For this series, the harmonic mean is 1% smaller than the arithmetic mean (Yule, 1911).

Mean age of cohort fertility, $M(T) = \Sigma(x^*g(x, T = t - x))/ \Sigma g(x, T = t - x)$

$m(t)$ is the time derivative of the mean age of fertility of the cohort which is age $A(t)$ in year t, where $A(t)$ is the mean age of period fertility.

$(1 - m(t))$ is the translation multiplier.

Appendix 3. Components of the quantum of cohort fertility

The progression ratio for parity zero, $R(0) = G(1)$.
The progression ratio for parity $y (= 1, 6)$ is defined as follows:
$R(y) = G(y + 1)/G(y)$ where $G(y) = \Sigma g(x, y)$.

An average progression ratio for parities $7+$ may be estimated as follows:

$G(8) = G(7)^*R(7)$; $G(9) = G(8)^*R(8)$, and so forth.
If $R(7) = R(8) = \ldots = R(7+)$,
  then $G(8) + G(9) + \ldots = (R(7+)^*G(7)) + (R^2(7+)^*G(7))$
  $+ \ldots$ and $(R(7+))/(1 - R(7+)) = (G(8+))/(G(7))$ giving
  $R(7+) = G(8+)/G(7+)$.

The cohort total fertility rate $G = G(1) + G(2) + G(3) + \ldots$
  $= R(0) + (R(0)^*R(1)) + (R(0)^*R(1)^*R(2)) + \ldots$

$$= \prod_{j=0}^{0} R(j) + \prod_{j=0}^{1} R(j) + \prod_{j=0}^{2} R(j) + \ldots$$

$$= \sum_{k=0}^{m-1} \prod_{j=0}^{k} R(j)$$

where n is the maximum order of birth.

Although this expression may look somewhat ponderous, it is in fact isomorphic with one of the most familiar measures in demography, the expectation of life at birth. If one defines $X(0) = {}_1L_0$ and $S(x) = {}_1L_x/{}_1L_{x-1}$ for $x = 1, w - 1$, where w is the maximum age at death,

$$\text{then} \quad {}_1L_x = \prod_{j=0}^{x} S(j) \text{ and } e_o = \sum_{x=0}^{w-1} {}_1L_x = \sum_{x=0}^{w-1} \prod_{j=0}^{x} S(j).$$

In words, the expectation of life at birth is the sum of a chain of progressively compounded age progression (survival) probabilities, whereas the total fertility rate is the sum of progressively compounded parity progression probabilities. The distinction between them is that the total fertility rate is a pure measure of quantum (of fertility) whereas the expectation of life at birth is a pure measure of tempo (of mortality)—since the quantum of mortality is uninteresting (everyone dies) and the only dimension is the time (age) of death.

G is decomposed into its low-parity and high-parity components as follows:

$$G = (R(0) + (R(0)*R(1)) + (R(0)*R(1)*R(2)) +$$
$$(R(0)*R(1)*R(2)*R(3)) + \ldots$$
$$= L + L^2 + (L^2*H) + (L^2*H^2) + \ldots$$
$$= L(1 + (L/(1 - H)))$$
Then $H = (G - G(1) - G(2))/(G - G(1))$
and $L = (((1 - H)/2)^2 + (2*G*(1 - H)/2))^{0.5} - ((1 - H)/2).$

Appendix 4. Components of the tempo of cohort fertility

The problem of estimating interval length from the available data may be posed as follows. We can calculate for each cohort the mean age at occurrence of the yth birth, $M(y) = \sum x*g(x, y)/\sum g(x, y)$.

Yet one cannot take serious the value $(M(y + 1) - M(y))$ as an estimate of the yth interval, that from the yth to the $y + 1$th birth, because there are two kinds of yth birth—those which are followed by a $y + 1$th birth, with a mean of $M'(y)$, and those which are not, with a mean of $M''(y)$, and $M''(y)$ is ordinarily different from $M'(y)$.

The assumption we propose is a convenient one, and has a ring of plausibility: $M''(y) = M(y + 1)$.

Accordingly we have

$$M(y) = (R(y)*M'(y)) + (1 - R(y))*M''(y)$$
$$= (R(y)*M'(y)) + (1 - R(y))*M(y + 1)$$

and $I(y) = M(y + 1) - M'(y)$
$$= (M(y + 1) - M(y))/R(y)$$

There are some data with which we can test this estimate. From the data of the 1965 National Fertility Study, for c.1911–20, the estimate for $I(1)$ was 1% greater than the observed value, the estimate for $I(2)$ was 1% less than the observed value, and the estimate for $I(3)$ was 13% less than the observed value. None of the differences was significant at the 95% level (Nordberg, 1975). From the 1970 Census, for Whites and Negroes combined, for c.1920–24, the estimate for $I(1)$ was 4% less than the observed, and the estimate for $I(2)$ was 1% less than the observed. Likewise, for c. 1925–29, the estimate for $I(1)$ was 6% less than the observed, and the estimate for $I(2)$ was 4% less than the observed (US Bureau of the Census, 1970).

The estimation formula for $I(y)$ was used for $y = 1, 2, 3$. For the small number of higher order intervals, an average value, $I(4+)$, was determined in the following way.

$$G(5+)*I(4+) = (G(5)*I(4)) + (G(6)*I(5)) + \ldots$$
$$= (G(5)*M(5) - M(4))/R(4) + (G(6)*(M(6) - M(5))/R(5) + \ldots$$
$$= (G(4)*(M(5) - M(4)) + (G(5)*(M(6) - M(5)) + \ldots$$
$$= ((G(4)*M(5)) + (G(5)*M(6)) + \ldots) - ((G(4)*M(4)) + (G(5)*M(5)) + \ldots$$

Assume $R(4) = R(5) = \ldots = R(4+) = (G(5+)/(G(4+))$

Then $G(5+)*I(4)+) = (G(4+)*(M(5+) - M(4+))$ and $I(4+) = (M(5+) - M(4))/R(4+)$

With these data, the mean interbirth interval, I, is calculated:

$$I = (((G(2)*I(1)) + (G(3)*I(2)) + (G(4)*I(3)) + (G(5+)*I(4+)))/(G - G(1))$$

The principal purpose is the decomposition of M.

$$G*M = (G(1)*M(1)) + (G(2)*M(2)) + (G(3)*M(3)) + \ldots$$
$$M(2) = M(1) + (R(1)*I(1))$$
$$M(3) = M(1) + (R(1)*I(1)) + (R(2)*I(2)) + \ldots$$

Substituting, we have

$$M = M(1) + (I(1)*(R(1)*G(2+)/G)) + (I(2)*(R(2)*G(3+)/G)) + \ldots$$

The latter terms are obviously a weighted sum of interval lengths, suggesting that we can write: $M = M(1) + K*I$.
Then K is calculated as $K = (M - M(1))/I$.
To get an intuitive feeling for the determinants of K, we made the assumption that $R(y)$ and $I(y)$ were constant across orders. In that case,

$$G*M = (G(1)*M(1)) + (G(2)*M(2)) + \dots$$
$$= (G(1)*M(1)) + (G(2)*(M(1) + RI)) + (G(3)*(M(1) + 2RI)) + \dots$$

so that $M = M(1) + (I*R*(\phi - 1))$, where ϕ is the mean order of birth. Empirically we found a very close correspondence between K and $R(\phi - 1)$. For R, we used $G/(G + 1)$, which is derivative from $G = R + R^2 + R^3 + \dots$, implicit in the assumption of a constant $R(y)$ across orders. For ϕ, we used the formula

$$\phi = (\sum_{y=1}^{7} y*G(y)) + ((8 - (7*R(7+)))/((1 - R(7+))*G(8+)))/G,$$

where the coefficient of $G(8+)$ is derivative from the assumption of a fixed parity progression ratio for parities 7 and higher.

Appendix 5. Allocation of responsibility for movements of the period total fertility rate

(a) *Period total fertility rate as a function of cohort quantum and change in cohort tempo*
$F(t) = G(t)*d(t)$
In the expressions comparing parameters of two periods or cohorts, we will henceforth identify the earlier time with a single prime and the later with a double prime.
$$F'' - F' = ((G'' - G')*(d'' + d')/2) + ((d'' - d')*(G'' + G')/2)$$
For later use, the proportion of change in F attributable to change in G is $P(1) = ((G'' - G')(d'' + d'))/(2(F'' - F'))$; $Q(1) = 1 - P(1)$.

(b) *Cohort quantum as a function of the low-parity and high-parity components*
$$G(T) = L(T)*(1 + (L(T)/(1 - H(T)))). \text{ Let } (1/(1 - H(T))) = E(T)$$

$(G'' - G') = (L'' - L')*(1 + ((E' + E'')*(L' + L'')/2))$
$+ (H'' - H')*(E'*E''*(L'^2 + L''^2)/2$

For later use, the proportion of change in G attributable to change in L is $P(2) = (L'' - L')(2 + ((E' + E'')*(L' + L'')))$ $/(2*(G'' - G'))$; $Q(2) = 1 - P(2)$.

(c) Change in cohort tempo as a function of changes in mean age at first birth, mean length of interbirth interval, and interval scale factor

$M(T) = M(1, T) + (K(T)*I(T))$

$m = m(1) + kI + Ki$ where the lower-case letters signify the time-derivatives of the upper-case letters.

$(1 - m'') - (1 - m') = m' - m''$
$= (m(1)' - m(1)'') + (((k' - k'')*(I' + I'')) +$
$((K' - K'')*(i' + i'')))/2 + ((((i' - i''))*(K' + K''))$
$+ ((I' - I'')*(k' + k'')))/2$

For later use, the proportion of change in $(1 - m)$ attributable to change in the scale factor is $P(3, 1) = (((k' - k'')*(I' + I'')) +$ $((K' - K'')*(i' + i'')))/(2*(m' - m''))$.

The proportion of change in $(1 - m)$ attributable to change in the mean age at first birth is $P(3, 2) = (m(1)' - m(1)'')/(m' - m'')$.

The proportion of change in $(1 - m)$ attributable to change in the mean interbirth interval is $P(3, 3) = 1 - P(3, 1) - P(3, 2)$.

(d) Allocation of contributions

The direct division of responsibility for long-term movements in the period total fertility rate between cohort quantum, on the one hand, and change in cohort tempo, on the other, is that between $P(1)$ and $Q(1)$. However, there is an indirect effect of cohort quantum on change in cohort tempo, through the interval scale factor K. Thus the total quantum component is $P(1) + (Q(1)*P(3, 1))$, and the first term in this can be further subdivided into low-parity and high-parity pieces: $P(1)*P(2)$ and $P(1)*Q(2)$.

The total tempo component, subdivided into age at first birth and interbirth interval is $(Q(1)*P(3, 2)) + (Q(1)*P(3, 3))$.

It should be noted that not all forces operate in the same direction in any particular comparison of periods and cohorts. Accordingly, some values of P or Q may be less than zero, and some values may be greater than one.

References

GIBSON, C. (1977) The elusive rise in the American birthrate. *Science* **196**(4289), 500–503.

NORDBERG, OLIVIA S. (1975) Reproductive Behavior of the American Birth Cohort of 1911–1920. Ph.D. dissertation, Princeton University, October 1975, p.63.

RYDER, N.B. (1964) The process of demographic translation. *Demography* **1**(1), 74–82.

RYDER, N.B. (1965) The cohort as a concept in the study of social change. *American Sociological Review* **30**(6), 843–861.

US BUREAU OF THE CENSUS, Census of Population (1970) *Subject Reports*, Final Report PC(2)-3B, Childspacing and Current Fertility, US Government Printing Office, Washington, D.C., 1975, Tables 88–90.

WESTOFF, C.F., and N.B. RYDER (1977) The predictive validity of reproductive intentions. *Demography* **14**(4), 431–453.

YULE, G.U. (1911) *An introduction to the theory of statistics.* p.156. London: Charles Griffin.

RECENT TRENDS IN FERTILITY
IN WESTERN EUROPE

D. J. VAN DE KAA

Netherlands Interuniversity Demographic Institute

Introduction

As long as Western Europe remains populated, there will be 'recent trends' in vital events. However, there are both auspicious and inauspicious moments to talk about recent trends in fertility. And, in my view, the present moment is inauspicious. The reasons for this are the following:

(a) Fertility in Western Europe has now been declining for well over a decade. Given the speed of this decline one would expect the lower limits to come into view very soon. But, if an upturn is in the offing, there is as yet very little sign of it.

(b) Since the phenomenon of decline is no longer recent, quite a few demographers have already looked at it and they have done so from almost all conceivable angles. Reading through the documents published on the topic during the last half dozen years or so is, in fact, very similar to reading the fertility chapters in a text book.

(c) Adding something new under these circumstances requires either great efforts in data collection, for which the period around the end of a year is not very suitable, or going beyond the presentation and description of trends, which is difficult at the best of times.

The approach I intend to follow is a compromise between the two just mentioned. I shall begin with a presentation of trends between 1950 and the most recent dates for which information could be obtained without going to extreme lengths. I will then offer some thoughts on the processes in society which determine these trends.

Table 1.   Crude birth rates 1950–1977.

Country	1950	1955	1960	1965	1970	1975	1976	1977[a]
Belgium	16·8	16·8	17·0	16·5	14·8	12·2	12·3	12·4
Denmark	18·6	17·3	16·6	18·0	14·4	14·2	12·9	12·2
England and Wales	15·8	15·0	17·1	18·1	16·1	12·3	11·9	11·7
Federal Republic of Germany	16·5	16·0	17·4	17·7	13·4	9·7	9·8	9·4
Finland	24·5	21·2	18·5	17·1	14·0	14.1	14·0	13·9
France	20·5	18·5	17·9	17·8	16·8	14·1	13·6	14·0
The Netherlands	22·7	21·3	20·8	19·9	18·3	13·0	12·9	12·5
Norway	19·1	18·5	17·3	17·8	16·6	14·1	13·3	12·6
Sweden	16·5	14·8	13·7	15·9	13·7	12·7	12·0	11·6
Switzerland	18·1	17·1	17·6	18·8	15·8	12·3	11·7	11·5

[a] Provisional figures

Source: Official Statistical Publications and/or yearbooks, personal communication.

Trends in period measures

Trends in the birth rate and its components

The frequency of births in the populations of Western and Northern Europe is now mostly in the order of 11–14 per thousand. It is only in one instance, the Federal Republic of Germany, that a significantly lower level (9·4 per thousand) occurs (table 1).

The present level is, without a single exception, substantially lower than in 1950, but in the path followed to that level some variation is noticeable. In the countries where the birth rates in 1950 were highest (Finland, the Netherlands and France), the decline has been almost continuous, although usually less pronounced before than after the mid-1960s. In all other cases the birth rates increased from the mid-fifties to the mid-sixties but decreased sharply thereafter (figure 1).

The decline since 1975 has been fairly uniform, an acceleration at the beginning of this decade being apparent in a number of cases. Finland is the only country where the birth rate has increased significantly in the last few years. If one has a sufficiently rich imagination, the 1976 or 1977 figures for Belgium and France could, however, be interpreted as the first signs of an imminent change of course.

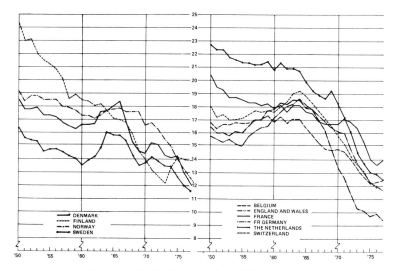

Figure 1.   Crude birth rate (per 1 000 population).

Since the crude birth rate is not a fully satisfactory measure of period fertility, a good deal of effort has been devoted to calculations aimed at isolating the effect of various structural factors influencing the frequency of births in a population. Berent and Festy (1973) have done so for a substantial number of countries in the ECE-region, while Frinking has covered most of the countries which are members of the Council of Europe. The results of these calculations show that, with a few exceptions and during brief periods, the changing sex–age structure has had a negative effect on the birth rate. In those countries, where the birth rate was increasing during the periods 1960–1964 and/or 1965–1969 (Belgium, Federal Republic of Germany, Switzerland, England and Wales) the increase would thus have been even more marked if the moderating effect of the sex–age structure had not occurred.

Nuptiality has, ' . . . on the whole (had) a continuously buoyant effect . . . in Northern and Western Europe but' . . . more so in the early post-war years than recently (United Nations, 1975, II, p.91). The increasing marriage rates, mainly due to a lowering of the average age at marriage and a decline in celibacy would, in fact, have led to an increase in the birth rates up till the late 1960s, if after about 1964 the decline in marital fertility had not more than

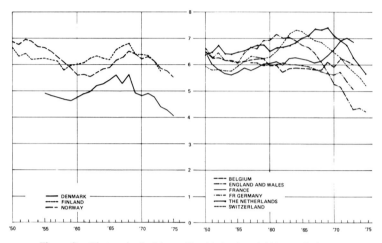

Figure 2.   First-order legitimate live births (per 1 000 population).

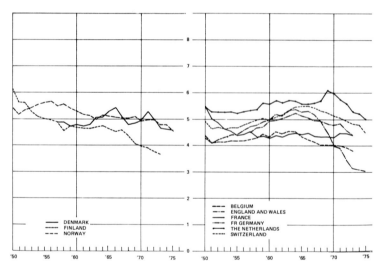

Figure 3.   Second-order legitimate live births (per 1 000 population).

offset the further increase in nuptiality up to the late 1960s. After the late 1960s, the decline in marital fertility has, in general, been reinforced by a decline in nuptiality. This partly explains the acceleration in the decrease of the birth rate since about 1970 noted earlier.

Trends by birth order

The developments just described gain further relief if the birth rates are analysed by order. The first order legitimate birth rates presented in figure 2 show a picture of increased variation since 1950, the differences around 1975 being quite marked. In most instances an increase to a given year is followed by a decline. In four countries (Finland, Denmark, Norway and the Netherlands) this year is 1968/1969 and in the northern countries this coincides with increased fertility outside marriage. The picture for Western Europe as a whole gives the impression of a group of countries going through the same sequence of events but being slightly out of step with one another. The suggestion implied is, of course, that these events relate to changes in the age at marriage, and the frequency of marriage as well as to the process of family building within marriage.

The graphs of second-order births in Western Europe (figure 3) do

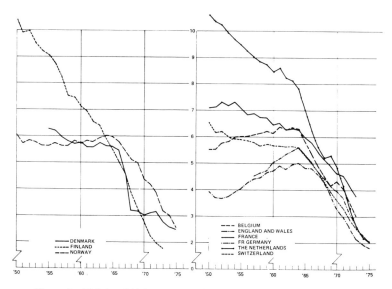

Figure 4.   Third and higher order legitimate live births (per 1 000 population).

not resemble a 'cat-o'-nine tails' as beautifully as the previous set, although a certain increase in variation is apparent. On the whole, however, the changes are less drastic and the peak is centred more uniformly around the mid-sixties. Figure 4 gives a very vivid impression of the changes which occurred in the rates for third and higher order births. In some respects the graphs give a greatly amplified version of those for the birth rate as a whole.

The decline in Finland, the Netherlands and France, for example, is continuous. What is most striking, however, is the remarkably sharp decline after 1964, which was only in a few cases preceded by a certain increase. Third and higher order births are now only fairly rarely born, the frequency of such births in the population having declined to no more than 2 or 3 per thousand.

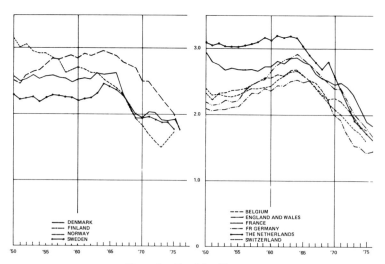

Figure 5.   Total fertility rate.

Trends by age of mother
The changes in the total fertility rate over the period 1950–1975 in the ten countries are by no means as volatile as those in the crude birth rate (figure 5). The general pattern is, nevertheless, similar. In most of the West European countries the rates increase from the early 1950s to 1964 reaching a peak at levels between 2·6 to 2·8 children per woman. In the Nordic countries and the Netherlands,

the changes between 1950 and 1964 are not very substantial, but after 1964 they experience the same strong decline.

Analysis of the changes in the age components of the total fertility rate throws some further light on the type of processes involved.

Fertility amongst women younger than 25 years of age rose in practically all countries between 1950 and the mid-sixties, sometimes rather steeply (Federal Republic of Germany, England and Wales). At that time women under 25 contributed between 0·8 and 1·15 child to the total fertility rate in all countries. This figure has now declined to 0·55 in the Netherlands, Switzerland and the Federal Republic of Germany but is higher elsewhere (figure 6).

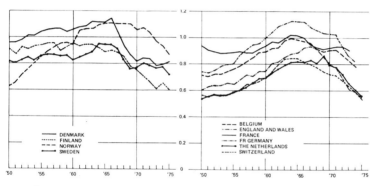

Figure 6.   Contribution to total fertility rate by women under 25 years of age

The age group 25–29, which is not separately shown here, follows the pattern just described in a general sense, but the fluctuations are much more subdued. It is further clear that the differences between the countries involved are not very great. The graphs for the individual countries tend to move more or less parallel in a narrow band.

With regard to women aged 30 and more, a striking, though no longer surprising, pattern emerges. Except for a few countries, where the contribution of women aged 30 years and over remained largely constant up till the mid-sixties, the picture is one of continuous decline, strongly so after 1964. Women aged 30+ now contribute not more than between 0·4 and 0·5 of a child to the total

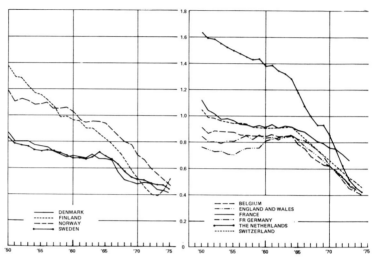

Figure 7.   Contribution to total fertility rate by women 30 years and
older.

fertility rate in nine of the countries. The analysis demonstrates
again the disappearance of higher order births and the movement
towards childbearing during a short period at a relatively young
age.

Trends by duration of marriage

There are not very many European countries where births are, or
can be, calculated by birth order and marriage duration. Material
of this type is, however, very valuable in detecting changes in the
tempo and rate of childbearing. When the ECE-secretariat carried
out its study in 1974 it proved possible, for example, to establish by
comparing the marriage cohorts of 1948, 1953, 1958 and 1963, that
' . . . both the total proportion of women experiencing a first birth
and the rate at which first births accumulated rose uniformly from
the marriage cohort of 1948 to that of 1963 in most countries'
(United Nations, 1975, II, p.106). The situation for second births was
found to be very similar. With regard to third and fourth births the
picture was more complicated and difficult to document, but the
general impression was one of a fairly monotonous decline both in
tempo and quantum from the older to the younger cohorts.

If the figures are extended in time and are also calculated for the

NORWAY   ------ MARRIAGE COHORT 1953   THE NETHERLANDS
          ───── MARRIAGE COHORT 1963
          ── ── MARRIAGE COHORT 1968

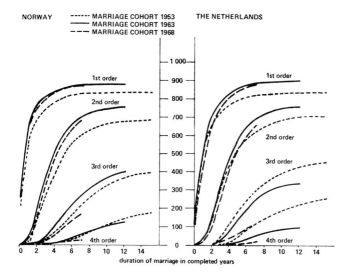

duration of marriage in completed years

FEDERAL REPUBLIC GERMANY   BELGIUM

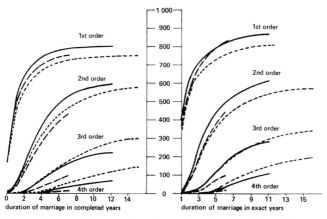

Figure 8. Cumulative marital fertility by duration of marriage and
   birth-order for selected marriage cohorts, four selected countries.

1968 marriage cohort, a very different pattern emerges (figure 8). It
is evident that, as far as first and second births are concerned, from
the 1963 to the 1968 marriage cohorts a reversal of trends has

Table 2.   Pre-marital conceptions per 100 marriages.

Country	Marriages concluded about:			
	1955	1960	1965	1970
Belgium	16	16	19	19
Denmark	31	33	34	21
England and Wales	13	16	20	18
Federal Republic of Germany		29	28	28
Finland	36	36	36	33
France	18	19	22	26
The Netherlands	17	17	19	18
Sweden	32	31	33	25
Switzerland	24	26	29	25

Source: Prioux-Marchal, 1974, Table I.

occurred. In the countries selected, the 1968 curves for these rank-numbers tend to lie between those for the cohorts of 1953 and 1963, or even below them. The decline in third and fourth births appears to have continued in all cases. It may be concluded that the trend towards younger childbearing has come to a halt and that first and second birth intervals are lengthening. At the same time, child-bearing remains concentrated during a short period of the total reproductive span.

Trends in extra-marital conceptions and extra-marital fertility

In 1974 Prioux-Marchal published a paper which contained an analysis of pre-nuptial conceptions in Western Europe since 1955. Using data to some extent especially obtained from central statistical offices, she was able to study the frequency of births in the first seven months of marriage by age of mother and to extend this study generally to marriages concluded in 1971. Table 2, taken from her paper, shows that the proportion of pre-marital conceptions remained quite stable over time, but that around 1970 a substantial decline occurred in both Sweden and Denmark.

Festy (1976) has recently extended the analysis for almost the same group of countries to 1974. The changes reported during these few additional years are very striking. The proportion of pregnant brides has declined sharply in the Netherlands, England and Wales, and the Federal Republic of Germany. The figures for Sweden and

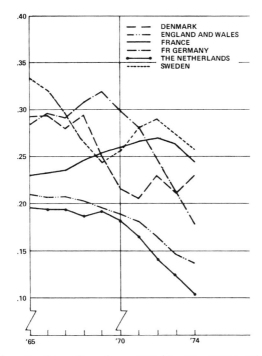

Figure 9. Proportions of pregnant brides. Source: Festy (1976).

Denmark fluctuate since about 1970, while in France a decline cannot be discerned until 1972. Festy further established that the proportion of extra-marital conceptions legitimated by marriage before the birth of a child is declining in all countries studied. In the Netherlands, the Federal Republic of Germany, France and England and Wales, where these proportions ranged from 75 to 45 in 1974, this decline is not spectacular. In Sweden and Denmark, however, the decline between 1965 and 1974 has been very strong; from 55 to less than 15 in the first case and from about 60 to about 35 in the second. One of the most stimulating aspects of Festy's contribution to the discussion of recent fertility trends in Western Europe is that he illustrates the remarkable contrast in the relationship between the changes in marriage pattern and the frequency of illegitimate conception in the Nordic countries Sweden and Denmark on the one hand, and West European countries such as the Netherlands and England and Wales on the other.

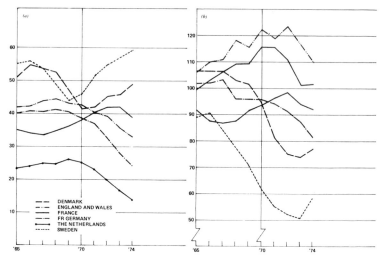

Figure 10.   (a) Illegitimate conception rate (per 1 000 unmarried women
aged 15–49).
(b) Marriages of females 15–49 (per 1 000 unmarried women).
Source: Festy (1976).

In Sweden and Denmark the number of marriages per thousand
unmarried women has declined fairly strongly from about 1966 to
1973. In England and Wales and in the Netherlands the rates
increased up till the early 1970s and declined thereafter. As far as
the illegitimate conception rate is concerned a decline from 1966 to
about 1969, followed by an increase, is the pattern in Sweden and
Denmark. In England and Wales, in the Netherlands and the
Federal Republic of Germany the pattern is one of decline from
1970 onward. Also, in Festy's view, this contrast may be indicative
of a difference in phase of an essentially similar sequence of events.
It should finally be noted that, largely as a result of these differences in trends, the proportion of illegitimate births in Western
Europe around 1975 varies widely, from well over 32% in Sweden
to not more than about 2% in the Netherlands.

Discussion

The interpretation of the trends

In historical demography people frequently have to be content
with rather incomplete time series of simple period measures as an

indication of changes in demographic trends. By studying these and by placing them in a broader historical setting they tend to arrive at ingenious and convincing theories as to the nature of the processes underlying these changes. Nowadays, time series of period measures can usually be supplemented by cohort or generation data. Such additional information will, in many instances, be extremely useful and is sometimes indispensable, e.g. when one wants to make an estimate of the completed family size of currently fertile couples. However, there is usually a time lag of several years between period and cohort data. Moreover, arranging data by cohort tends to smooth out the effects of fairly abrupt changes in behaviour (see Blayo and Festy, 1975), which may be a disadvantage if the explanation of these changes is the main point of interest. Therefore, since the focus of this paper is on recent trends in fertility and the interpretation of their largely unexpected rise and fall before and after the mid-sixties it is probably not a serious handicap that our attention will have to remain limited mainly to the period measures just presented.

What do they show? Looking a little beyond them it is clear that the fertility indices reflect important changes in reproduction and family formation in Western Europe. It would appear that after the immediate postwar years, the average age at marriage started to decline. At the same time the proportions ever-marrying increased and so did the frequency of remarriage. It is likely that the family size norms existing at the time were the same as, or very similar to, those adhered to by the cohorts marrying around the 1930s. But while due to very adverse economic conditions the latter groups may have been forced to restrict the size of their families below the level desired, people marrying around the fifties experienced a period of rapid economic growth and will thus have been able to achieve higher fertility within marriage. The decline in the age at first marriage just indicated may have been associated with an increase in the frequency of pre-marital sexual relations and with a lowering of the age at which such relations began. However, having sexual relations outside marriage was not widely accepted, certainly not as far as women were concerned, and obtaining official sanction through marriage remained the norm and the solution in case of a pre-marital conception.

At first, concluding a marriage did not only indicate a couple's readiness or desire to receive official sanction to live together, but it also indicated the couple's readiness to 'start a family'. The average age of fertility declined, the interval between marriage and a first birth remained short, the birth rates for the lower rank numbers started to rise and fertility during the early parts of the reproductive period increased. The use of contraception to limit the size of completed families became generally accepted, but the means and methods were not perfect and their use probably suited experienced couples most. Gradually, the automatism between marrying and the commencement of childbearing loosened. Pre-marital sexual relations were mostly still frowned upon and marriage was still desired as a sign of official approval, but it was no longer indicative of being mentally and materially ready to raise children. The use of contraception for planning purposes early in married life became more popular, which allowed a further decline in the age of marriage. Just about that time new and highly effective means of contraception became available and were readily adopted in many countries. First and second birth intervals lengthened, the frequency of lower-order births decreased, and the size of completed families became relatively rigidly controlled. Due also, undoubtedly, to changes in family size norms, fertility at ages above 30 years declined very sharply and the birth of children with higher ranknumbers became an exception. The frequency of lower-order births in the population further declined because (pending) changes in abortion legislation in many countries made it either *de jure* or *de facto* possible to terminate unwanted pre-marital conceptions. The gradual disappearance of 'forced marriages' reduced the decline in the age at first marriage or started to reverse the trend. Abortion could, similarly, be used to prevent within marriage the birth of unwanted children of higher ranknumbers or births to mothers at a somewhat more advanced age. The increased adoption of sterilization as a means of controlling fertility in completed families further reduced the number of higher order births.

Once the proposition that sexual relations in marriage were not solely or primarily aimed at procreation had become generally accepted and contraceptives of high quality had become available, a further step was set in at least a number of countries. The need to seek an official sign of approval before starting to live together was questioned and stable unions were formed. Since neither early marriage nor young unions were entered into in order to have children, the difference between them was, in practice, indeed not much more than a paper certificate. This the more so because marriage itself became a much less permanent arrangement. The frequency of divorce rose and divorce started, on average, to occur earlier in marriage.

It is likely that there must, at least initially, have been some pressure on people in 'non-paper marriages' to marry once the birth of a child was desired or announced itself. In certain countries this pressure is now apparently reduced to such an extent that the need to marry before starting a family is no longer felt. In such countries the trend in the age at first marriage is reversed, and (re)marriage rates decline. Illegitimate birth rates increase, while the proportions of ex-nuptial conceptions legitimated by marriage decline. Voluntary childlessness is no longer solely an option for men and women who elect not to marry. The decline in total fertility rate starts to slow down.

Three interesting questions now arise. The first is, whether there is evidence in addition to the time series on fertility with which the occurrence of the events just described can be documented; the second whether it can be shown that they occur in a certain relation, or better, sequence to each other; the third, whether such a possible chain of events is likely to occur in all countries of Europe.

The answer to the first question can, no doubt, be affirmative. There is a very large amount of information, some of it already quoted, which can be used to document the events listed. Only some of it, meant to illustrate a number of specific points, will be referred to here. In a recent publication on sexual behaviour amongst the young, Geeraert (1977, p.27) cites a long list of similar empirical research in western countries since 1900 and concludes that, particularly amongst young women, both those studying and working, pre-marital coitus has become increasingly common. For example, in 1971 the proportion of 21 year old working youngsters in Western Germany who had experienced pre-marital coitus reached 83% amongst both males and females. In Denmark the proportion of 21 year old female students who had had pre-marital sexual relations increased from 60% in 1958 to 97% in 1968. For the Netherlands Kooy (1975, p.140) reports that of men and women, born in 1903–1918 57 and 32% respectively had experienced pre-marital sexual relations. For men and women born in 1943–1947 these figures had risen to 85 and 70% respectively. A table on the pre-marital sexual experience of women by period of, and age at, first marriage published by Grebenik (OPCS, 1977, p.57) for Great Britain confirms these changes strikingly.

The changes in age at marriage, and in proportions marrying and remarrying in Western Europe have recently been reviewed in the drafts of two documents to be published by the Council of Europe (Kirk, 1977; Roussel & Festy, 1977), probably sometime in 1978. They leave no doubt that in most countries marriages have never been so frequent and so early as for the cohorts born around 1940. They also show that the decline in the age at first marriage is coming to an end in the Netherlands, for example, and that in the late 1960s first marriage rates fell rather steeply in Denmark, Sweden and the Federal Republic of Germany, with Norway, England and Wales, and Switzerland following in the early 1970s. In some countries (Sweden, Switzerland) remarriage rates follow the pattern of first marriages closely; in others (England and Wales) the similarity in trend is not obvious. The decline in the average age of fertility in developed countries has, at least until the early 1970s, been well documented by Campbell (1973), while all figures on the mean age of mothers presented in the United Nations publication on the ECE-countries (United Nations, 1975, table V.7) for the countries of Western Europe show a decline of sometimes more than three years if data for 1950 are compared with the latest available. Survey data for 6 of the countries now selected and contained in another UN publication (1976) provide information on the intervals between successive births. A comparison of marriage cohorts before 1951, 1951–1955, 1956–1960 and 1961–1965 shows a very marked increase in the proportion of expected family size achieved during the first six years of marriage. The proportions for the cohort before 1951 range from 39 in Finland to 52 in Belgium and France. For the cohort 1961–1965 they range from 59 in Denmark to 82 in England and Wales, figures which are illustrative of both the narrowing of the period used for reproduction and, in the case of Denmark, the postponement of lower order births. Detailed figures presented by Frinking (1975, table B) for France, Belgium and the Netherlands show an increase in the mean duration of the interval between marriage and a first birth since 1964 in all cases. From 1·772 years to 1·850 years in 1973 for France, from 1·851 to 1·995 in 1972 for Belgium and from 1·755 to 2·274 in 1973 for the Netherlands. Such changes are apparently shared by Norway, Denmark, England and Wales and the Federal Republic.

The use of contraception before and after marriage has been surveyed extensively in Western Europe. The UN publication cited earlier (1976) presents data on 'current users' around 1970. As a percentage of all respondents the figures range from 64 in France to 77 in Finland. As a percentage of respondents exposed to the risk of pregnancy values of close to 85% appear to be common. Even so, the methods and means used differ widely. In France and Belgium more than 50% practised withdrawal, while this figure reached about a quarter in England and Wales and Finland. The pill and condoms accounted for 66% in Finland, 67% in Denmark, 29% in France, 14% in Belgium, 60% in England and Wales and 68% in the Netherlands. Using additional sources, Glass (1976, table 8) has also tabulated the extent of contraceptive practice in a number of developed countries and the type of contraception used, with comparable results. Changes over time can sometimes be ascertained by comparing successive surveys, marriage cohorts or both. A national survey carried out in the Netherlands in 1975 showed a substantial increase in the proportion who ever used an efficient method of contraception when moving from the 1963−64 to the 1971−73 marriage cohort. Of all women married in 1963−64 59% ever used the pill; this proportion reached 72% for women married in 1971−73. The use of the rhythm method and withdrawal declined sharply, while sterilization proved to be the method applied by 10% of women (husbands) married in 1963−64 (Moors *et al.*, 1976).

The shift in planning strategy leading to long first birth intervals can be demonstrated with data presented by Moors (1976) and here reproduced in table 3. Moors has developed a family building typology based on factual information on planning behaviour during the first few years of marriage. The two types which interest us here, 'rational I' and 'rational II' both denote a careful type of planning but differ with regard to behaviour during the first years of marriage. People following rational I deliberately start a family immediately after marriage and practice effective planning as soon

Table 3.   Percentage distributions of first marriages by family
building pattern and marriage cohort (The Netherlands,
NOVOM, 1975).

	1963/4	1965/67	1968/70	1971/73
Subfecundity	19	19	19	19
Traditional	3	2	1	2
Hedonistic	11	9	10	12
Reaction	16	13	14	14
Rational I	43	45	40	26
Rational II	8	12	16	27

Source: Moors (1977) Table 6.

as the desired family size is reached. People choosing rational II postpone childbearing deliberately until later in marriage and plan effectively to achieve the desired size and spacing. It is evident from Moors' table that the shift to the rational II type has been quite strong in the Netherlands. For the same country data could also be quoted to show the recent very marked increase in sterilization as a means of family limitation (16 000 sterilizations in 1972 – 62 000 in 1975, equally divided by sex, 84 000 in 1976, 39 000 men and 45 000 women) and the impact of abortion on the frequency of forced marriages and the like. However, it is probably wiser to devote the remaining space to a few observations on divorce.

This topic has just been treated very fully for nine out of ten of the countries here considered, in a book edited by Chester (1977). In the conclusion of this book he presents a graph showing the frequency of divorce per thousand married women or thousand existing marriages, for all countries from 1945 onward. Notwithstanding variations in timing and level, the overwhelming impression is one of deeply U-shaped curves with levels in the mid-seventies approaching those in the immediate postwar years. This implies that divorce rates have doubled or tripled since the late 1960s in almost all countries, in particular in those where more liberal legislation has become in force (The Netherlands, 1971; England and Wales, 1970; Sweden, 1973). However, also in these countries, rising rates and increases in the frequency of divorce at fairly short durations of marriage existed well before then. The same phenomena are observed if other measures of divorce are used (Festy & Prioux, 1975).

Since relatively full data on changes in ex-nuptial pregnancies, illegitimacy and cohabitation have already been presented in the previous section, the stage is reached at which it can be concluded that it is undoubtedly possible to substantiate the claim that a large number of very significant events influencing fertility and family formation occurred in a smaller or greater number of countries of Western Europe since about 1950.

We must now turn to the second question, and ask whether these events are interrelated and form a chain. That they are interrelated is, of course, extremely likely. That they form a chain, a logical sequence, seems to be a sound working hypothesis, which cannot now be substantiated. Although it is tempting to formulate bold conclusions in this regard and to suggest distinct phases, this is almost certainly too early †. There are several reasons for this. One is that the interrelations between the various events are so complex and the variations in level and pattern from country to country such that, establishing an exact order, well-defined clusters, crucial levels or distinct turning points is no easy matter. As long as this has not been carefully done, it remains uncertain how features possibly unique for one country can be distinguished from those of a more general nature. Another is that, where so many changes and phenomena occur in a short period of time, there is bound to be such a degree of overlap and intertwining that the direction of the relationship tends to remain uncertain. A further point is that the whole range of events described has (so far) only occurred in a few countries, more specifically in Sweden and Denmark.

The various graphs do suggest a sequence of events through which countries are moving at somewhat different speed, but while certain events are well-defined in time (decline in birth rate in 1964) others (change in marriage and divorce patterns) are not similarly centred around one specific year. All this leads to a situation where one must conclude that the case for the existence of a well-defined sequence of events, can probably best be argued by making it plausible that the events in the various countries have common determinants. This brings us at the same time to the third question,

---

† Roussel & Festy (1977) distinguish and describe four phases. They do not, however, date them or indicate the duration of these phases for individual countries or for certain groups among them.

since it is reasonable to assume that in a group of countries the same series of demographic events will only occur if these countries share the determinants.

Determinants and consequences

To summarize the developments in West European societies since about 1950 in one sentence is obviously very risky. But challenged to do so, one might simply say: They have become more progressive! In a philosophical sense the term 'progressive' denotes a state of mind characterized by a tendency to accept the new sympathetically, to look at the present critically, and to have relatively little regard for the past. Progressiveness can be contrasted with conservatism, which reflects a state of mind characterized by a tendency to stress the value of traditions and to oppose changes[†]. As used here the term 'progressive' is meant to indicate a direction of change in which the fairly general and abstract values 'equality' and 'freedom' as already voiced during the French Revolution are increasingly emphasized[‡]. However, the emphasis they receive in different spheres of life is not the same. In the socio-economic sphere freedom is, from the progressive point of view, seen as a potential danger to equality, and where a conflict between the two arises 'equality' usually prevails over 'freedom'. To achieve equality, solidarity is called for and expected. In the socio-cultural sphere the opposite tends to be the case. As long as one's behaviour does not interfere with the freedom of others to act freely, one is free to behave as one sees fit. Different forms of behaviour are considered to be of equal value, even though this will lead to considerable pluriformity.

In summary, the progressive point of view stresses the equality of opportunities (income, education etc.) and freedom of choice in behaviour (dress, sexual behaviour etc.) It can easily be seen that the first line of approach stimulates the growth of the welfare state

---

[†] In the demagogy of politics the opposite terms 'progressive' and 'reactionary' are frequently used. While very many and very different parties will lay claim to the first designation, very few will accept the second.

[‡] The choice of the term 'progressive', therefore, does not in itself reflect a value judgement of the author. Whether objective criteria can be established to distinguish progressive and regressive tendencies in history is another, obviously rather difficult question (see Dooyeweerd, 1958).

and its distributive functions. The proportions of national income spent in the collective sector have, in fact, risen sharply and now reach values in the order of 20% in several West European countries (Van de Kaa, 1977). The second line of approach stimulates changes in collective and individual attitudes in many fields, including those regarding fertility and family formation. In the Netherlands these changes have been investigated by Middendorp (1974, 1975). Using a definition of 'progressiveness' as formulated above and survey data collected and kept in data archives, he has studied cultural change in the Netherlands during two periods, 1965–1970 and 1970–1974. For the period 1965–1970 three groups of questions could be studied. Twelve questions dealt with changes of opinion in political matters, ten with changes of opinion in the field of religion, and ten dealt with marriage, the family and sexuality. The movement towards greater progressiveness in the first two fields proved to be fairly limited. The proportion of respondents giving a progressive answer tended to increase by 5 to 20% but as a whole it can not be said that the shifts in opinion were very substantial. The changes in answers concerning the social security system were, in fact, not all in the same direction.

A completely different picture emerges when questions on marriage, the family, and sexuality are considered. These shifts in the direction of greater progressiveness reached magnitudes of 25 to 30% between the various surveys considered. Changes in opinion were particularly strong with regard to questions relating to: voluntary childlessness, participation in the labour force of married women, divorce, pornography, and abortion. For example, abortion was considered acceptable under certain circumstances by 58% of the respondents in 1968 and by 79% in 1970. In 1965 roughly 82% considered labour force participation of married women undesirable; in 1970 this proportion had declined to 43%.

The changes between 1970 and 1974 could only be studied by using six political questions and seven questions concerning marriage, the family and sexuality. The first group of answers showed an overall picture of great stability. Moreover, in 5 out of 6 cases, the shift was in the direction of greater conservatism. As opposed to this the answers to questions on marriage, the family and sexuality displayed a further movement towards progressiveness, although the shifts were much more limited than during 1965–1970.

What appears to be a crucial element from a demographic point of view in the changes noted, is that man–woman relations are increasingly seen as a means of reciprocal emotional enrichment to which the birth of children may, or may not, be considered to be contributing. The personal value, dignity and freedom of the individuals involved in such relations are often stressed, as are their rights to self-fulfilment. The relationships are expected to be based on love and mutual attraction, are entered into freely and come to an end once they are lastingly disrupted, the latter independent of whether they have the form of a stable union or a marriage. Marriage as an institution providing economic security and as an essentially permanent arrangement aimed at reproduction and enabling the rearing of children is no longer universally felt to be necessary.

It is possible, of course, that the expansion of secondary and higher education, particularly for women, and the increased participation of women in gainful employment, have increased their economic independence and will thus have facilitated the changes in man–woman relations. However, it would be very unwise not to recognize that the trend towards greater participation of women in the labour force and towards the emancipation of the sexes in many other fields, do themselves form part of the general shift towards greater progressiveness. One cannot, in fact, exclude with certainty the possibility that the real changes in the degree of economic independence of women were substantially smaller than the changes in opinions and attitudes, so that they limited rather than stimulated the changes in behaviour with regard to family formation and reproduction. It is interesting to note in this regard that a Danish research worker (Koch-Nielsen, 1978) asserts that a period of economic stagnation or a depression is likely to make marriage in that country more popular.

Data such as those presented by Middendorp and summarized in table 4 are difficult to interpret. But, if they are taken at face value they confirm the strong impressions which many social scientists in the Netherlands have voiced concerning the course of events in Dutch society since the end of World War 2. It is a course where the upheaval caused by the war was followed by a period of harmony and reconstruction lasting until the mid-sixties. In the 'radical sixties' a period of strong polarization followed (New Left) in

Table 4. Cultural changes regarding marriage, the family and sexuality (The Netherlands, 1965–1974).

Question on:	Proportion of respondents giving a progressive answer				
	1965	1966	1968	1970	1974[a]
1. The way children should address their parents	31.1	31.5	—	46.3	48·9
2. Whether a girl should remain a virgin until marriage	27·0	31·7	—	62·0	61·8
3. The acceptability of an infidelity on the part of the husband	20·3	—	—	45·5	48·8
4. The conditions under which abortion should be allowed	—	—	58·0	79·2	85·2
5. The acceptability of voluntary childlessness	21·8	27·2	—	59·4	64·7
6. The participation in the labour force of married women with school-going children	17·9	—	—	55·4	69·8
7. The tolerance in respect of homosexuals	—	—	56·4	69·1	83·8
N-size of sample	1302	1214	1274	1593	623

[a] Non-response reported to be unusually low.

Source: Middendorp, 1974 and 1975.

which various groups (Provos, Kabouters, Dolle Mina's, students) created unrest and voiced their protest against society and its norms. In political terms this movement subsided in the early 1970s; culturally speaking changes appear to continue, e.g. Women's Lib., emancipation of the sexes.

Although it would be rash to transpose the developments in the Netherlands to other settings, it is undeniable that student unrest has been a quite general phenomenon in Western Europe and that legislative changes concerning divorce, contraception, and abortion have been taken, or have been discussed and voted down, in many European countries at approximately the same time. It is worth noting in this regard that Simons (1977), in an attempt to find an exogenous explanation of recent fertility trends in England and Wales, seeks this explanation ' . . . . in terms of shifts in the relative appeal of two opposed sets of ideas (concerning childbearing), Fundamentalist and Pragmatist'. 'An essential characteristic of Fundamentalist thought is that it construes current behaviour and experience in terms of long established custom or eternal truths'; 'An essential characteristic of Pragmatist thought is that it construes current behaviour and experience in terms of its expected consequences', he writes. He then goes on to say that most real 'reproductive agents' will combine elements of the Fundamentalist or Pragmatist point of view, but that one set of ideas will always be dominant over the other, and makes two important suggestions. The first is, that the ideas of any real society ' . . . . can be placed somewhere on the Fundamentalist–Pragmatist axis,'. The second, that ' . . . independently of its position on the axis, a society can have a positive orientation towards either pole.'

These suggestions apply equally well to a progressive–conservative axis, and illustrate that Simons' and the present approach differ probably mainly in scope.

In returning to the present approach it may be observed that the 'progressive' and 'conservative' forces in the political field seem to hold each other roughly in balance in quite a few countries of Western Europe and that movements one way or the other are very small.

Demographers are not well placed to judge which direction the pendulum will ultimately go, or whether the movement will increase. Perhaps this is not too important. The data presented for the Netherlands suggest that small shifts in the weight of political parties, even though their political significance may be great, are not necessarily reflected in the opinions of the population on matters relating to marriage, the family and the like. And, since data on contraceptive practice, divorce etc. presented before, show that the scope for 'progressive changes' in many West European countries is still very considerable, it must be assumed that shifts in opinion and behaviour such as those observed recently will continue for some time to come. This is not to say that all West European countries will follow the example of Sweden and Denmark. Even though similar forces generate the change, they

Table 5. Estimated completed fertility, birth-cohort
1940.

Country	Number of children per woman
Belgium	2·23
Denmark	2·30
England and Wales	2·38
Federal Republic of Germany	1·99
Finland	2·10
France	2·49
The Netherlands	2·26
Norway	2·47
Sweden	2·07
Switzerland	2·11

Sources: Blayo and Festy, 1975; Delanghe and Dooghe, 1975; Sipponen and Hulkko, 1975.

may not everywhere have the same strength, exist for the same period or meet the same degree of opposition.

A few concluding remarks should now be made about the possible consequences of the continuation of cultural changes in society for future fertility trends. Two effects must probably be reckoned with. The erosion of third and higher order births is likely to be a fairly permanent feature and will affect the average numbers of children born per woman of the postwar birth cohorts. It is, similarly, likely that the birth of children will continue to occur only during a very limited period of the reproductive span. Figures, such as those presented in table 5 will thus, in many cases, present a maximum.

Changes in the timing of first and second births could conceivably continue in the same direction for a while, which would imply a continued low frequency of births in the population. However, there are no indications as yet that a return to the pattern of late childbearing, as displayed in the marriage cohorts of the late 1940s, is imminent. An increase in the frequency of births some time in the future thus becomes likely if the average family size desired by women and men of the younger birth cohorts does not decrease markedly. All that can be said in this regard is that survey results on this question continue to yield averages much in excess of current period measures.

Acknowledgement

The author gratefully acknowledges the very valuable assistance received from Mrs Jeannette Schoorl and Mrs Jacqueline Bakker in the collection and preparation of data and other material for this paper.

References

Unless otherwise stated the statistical data were obtained from official statistical publications or yearbooks.

BERENT, J. and FESTY, P. (1973). Measuring the impact of some demographic factors on post-war trends in CBR's in Europe. In *Proceedings International Population Conference, Liege 1973*, IUSSP, **II**, 99–112.

BLAYO, Ch. and FESTY, P. (1975). La fécondité à l'est et à l'ouest de l'Europe. *Population, 30*, 855–888.

CAMPBELL, A.A. (1973), The decline in average age of fertility in developed countries. In *Proceedings International Population Conference, Liege 1973*, IUSSP, **II**, 113–123.

CHESTER, R. (ed) (1977), *Divorce in Europe*, NIDI/CBGS-publications, No. 3, Martinus Nijhoff, Leyden, 316 pp.

DELANGHE, L. and DOOGHE, G. (1975), *Recente ontwikkelingen van het Belgisch vruchtbaarheidspatroon*, Brussels, CBGS-Technisch rapport no. 6, 71 pp.

DOOYEWEERD, H. (1958), The criteria of progressive and reactionary tendencies in history. *Verslav van de plechtige viering van het honderd-vijftigjarig bestaan der Koninklijke Nederlandse Akademie van Wetenschappen . . . ,* N.V. Noordhollandsche Uitgeversmaatschappij, Amsterdam, 213–228.

FESTY, P. (1976), *Extra marital fertility and its occurrence in stable unions; recent trends in Western Europe*, Second European Population Seminar, The Hague, 15 pp.

FESTY, P. and PRIOUX, F. (1975), Le divorce en Europe depuis 1950. *Population, 30*, 975–1017.

FRINKING, G.A.B. (1975), *Rapport sur les tendances recentes et futures de la fécondité en Europe occidentale*, La Haye, MS., 25 pp.

GEERAERT, A. (1977), *Sexualiteit bij jongeren*, Brussels, De Sikkel, De Nederlandse Boekhandel, 264 pp.

GLASS, D.V. (1976), Recent and prospective trends in fertility in developed countries. *Philosophical Transactions of the Royal Society of London.*, B. Biological Sciences, Vol. 274, No. 928, 1–52.

VAN DE KAA, D.J. (1977). The World Population Plan of Action and the welfare states of the Western World, In *Proceedings International Conference Mexico 1977*, IUSSP, **II**, 455–473.

KIRK, M. (1977), *The population situation and prospects in the member states of the Council of Europe*, Strasbourg, draft chapters 3 and 4.

KOCH-NIELSEN, I. (1978), *The future of marriage in Denmark,* DNISR, Booklet No. 7. Teknisk Forlag, Copenhagen, 44 pp.

KOOY, G.A. (1975), *Seksualiteit, huwelijk en gezin in Nederland*, van Loghum Slaterus, Deventer, 304 pp.

MIDDENDORP, C.P. (1974), Culturele veranderingen in Nederland, 1965–1970, *Intermediair, 10*, 15 maart.

MIDDENDORP, C.P. (1975), Verdere culturele veranderingen in Nederland? De periode 1970–1974. *Intermediair, 11*, 9 mei.

MOORS, H.G. (1977), Prognostische implicaties van de gezinsplanning in de eerste huwelijksjaren: het gebruik van survey-gegevens voor de schatting van de uiteindelijke gezinsgrootte, *Bevolking en Gezin*, No. 3, 361–384.
MOORS, H.G., VAN DONGEN, P.J.W.J., NIPHUIS-NELL, M. and DE VRIES, H. (1976), *Nationaal Onderzoek Vruchbaarheid en Ouderschapsmotivatie; Eerste resultaten.*, Voorburg, NIDI, Intern rapport no. 7, 35 pp.
PRIOUX-MARCHAL, F. (1974), Les conceptions pré-nuptiales en Europe occidentale depuis 1955, *Population*, **29**, 61–88.
OFFICE OF POPULATION CENSUSES AND SURVEYS (1978), *Demographic Review 1977*, HMSO, London, 100pp.
ROUSSEL, L. and FESTY, P. (1977), *Recent trends in attitudes and behaviour affecting the family in Council of Europe member states*, Strasbourg, draft paper, 59pp.
SIMONS, J. (1977). An interpretation of recent fertility trends in England and Wales, *British Regional Populations*, paper presented at a joint meeting of the British Society for Population Studies and the Institute of British Geographers, Liverpool, September 1977, 127–151.
SIPPONEN, K. and HULKKO, J. (1975), The population situation in Finland and the population policy it requires. In *Yearbook of Population Research in Finland 1975–76*; Helsinki, The Population Research Institute, pp. 9–16.
STATISTICAL OFFICE OF THE EUROPEAN COMMUNITIES, (1977), *Demographic Statistics, 1960–1976*, Brussels, 119 pp.
UNITED NATIONS (1975), *Postwar demographic trends in Europe and the outlook until the year 2000*. Part II of the Economic survey of Europe in 1974, New York, E.75.II.E.16. 252 pp.
UNITED NATIONS (1976), *Fertility and family planning in Europe around 1970: A comparative study of twelve national surveys*, New York, ST/ESA/SER. A/58, 180 pp.

RECENT TRENDS IN MARRIAGE AND DIVORCE IN BRITAIN AND EUROPE

D. A. COLEMAN

Department of Anthropology, University College, London

Introduction

Marriage is one of the more complex demographic phenomena and is also one of the less studied. This paper reviews changes in patterns of marriage and divorce since 1900 in England and Wales and in the context of the other countries of the West European tradition, suggests reasons for the changes and attempts to assess their significance. Data for England and Wales alone have been extensively analysed by Farid (1976) and Leete (1976, 1977a and in the press) so I will deal with more general and comparative aspects of marriage and divorce.

Data on the formation and breakdown of marriage, and their analysis, are in a less satisfactory state than those relating to mortality and fertility. Accurate and concise measures of marriage and divorce are relatively undeveloped, especially life-table approaches to duration of marriage, as opposed to nuptiality. This is partly due to the scarcity of data categorized in the appropriate way: for marriage studies this often needs to be categorized in rather elaborate ways. The married state may be entered at various ages and left at various ages, either by divorce or by death. Some will not enter it at all, others will enter it several times. Furthermore, in relation to marital fertility and to propensity to divorce, the partners' ages in combination and age differences need to be considered. The characteristics of remarriages, as opposed to first marriages, are largely unexplored.

Marriage trends in England and Wales

The great changes in mortality and fertility described as the

Table 1.   Mean age at first marriage, bachelors and spinsters, and the difference between the means. First marriages for both partners; England and Wales.

Year	Bachelors	Spinsters	Difference	Year	Bachelors	Spinsters	Difference
1951	26·14	23·50	2·64	1965	24·48	21·95	2·53
1952	26·06	23·41	2·65	1966	24·31	21·88	2·43
1953	25·90	23·27	2·63	1967	24·17	21·86	2·31
1954	25·84	23·18	2·66	1968	24·03	21·83	2·20
1955	25·72	23·16	2·66	1969	24·00	21·87	2·13
1956	25·58	22·92	2·66	1970	23·90	21·79	2·11
1957	25·46	22·80	2·66	1971	23·98	21·84	2·14
1958	25·32	22·68	2·64	1972	24·05	21·88	2·17
1959	25·22	22·58	2·64	1973	24·06	21·86	2·20
1960	25·12	22·48	2·64	1974	24·10	21·90	2·20
1961	25·04	22·38	2·66	1975	24·19	21·97	2·22
1962	24·97	22·29	2·68	1976	24·27	22·03	2·24
1963	24·85	22·17	2·68	1977	24·32	22·06	2·26
1964	24·69	22·06	2·63				

Sources: Marriage and Divorce Statistics. Series FM21, 1974 2, 1975 table 3.5b, Registrar-General's Statistical Review 1969 Part II Table 2, p. 61.

'demographic transition' took place within a very stable framework of marriage patterns. In Victorian times, bachelors and spinsters married late—around 28 and 26 years of age respectively. More than 10% never married at all. Even in 1901–1905 mean age at marriage for bachelors was 26·9 years and for spinsters 25.4. In 1901, 11% of men and 14% of women aged between 45 and 49 had never married—the normal pattern since the 17th century at least (Hajnal, 1965).

But by the 1930s a clear change in marriage patterns became apparent, gradually at first and then with greater speed after World War 2. This change marked the end of the clear distinction between the marriage patterns of Western Europe and those of the rest of the world. Average age at marriage declined, the proportions ever-married at given ages rose. Initially, marriage rates rose most among those aged over 30 years (Hajnal, 1947). Between 1936 and 1940, mean age at marriage for bachelors was 27·26, for spinsters 24·84. During the wartime quinquennium this fell to 26·34 and 23·81 respectively, and never recovered its previous level. In 1951 the mean ages were 26·14 and 23·50 respectively.

Table 1 shows that this decline was subsequently maintained in an approximately linear fashion; by 1970 mean age at marriage for bachelors had fallen by 2·24 years to 23·90 years, the lowest since records began; probably the lowest for three centuries. This represents a fall of 0·12 years per year since 1951. And by 1970, spinsters were marrying at average age 21·79, a fall of 1·71 years (0·09 years per annum). The differences between the mean ages declined, though not to begin with. 2·64 years separated the average bachelor groom from the average spinster bride in 1951, 2·68 years in 1963. All the decline to 2·11 years in 1970 occurred after 1963; bachelors' mean age at marriage fell most rapidly after 1963 while most of the fall in spinsters' age at marriage occurred before this date.

As mean age at marriage falls towards the minimum age, its distribution becomes even more skewed and the mean accordingly becomes a less sensitive indicator of nuptiality change. Age-specific marriage rates (figure 1) show the postwar change in marriage more dramatically. The data show both a shift forward in the most popular ages at marriage, and a general increase in nuptiality. Proportions ever-married have consequently increased in successive years, so that the proportion ever-married at earlier ages exceeds the level previously attained at considerably older ages, especially among women. For example, among men the proportion married at age 30−34 in 1951 (31·0%) was about the same as that among men aged 35−39 (31·4%) in 1911, and the proportion of men ever-married by their early thirties (30−34) in the peak year

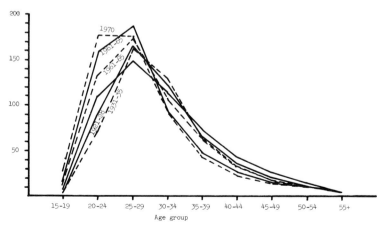

Figure 1. England and Wales 1921−1970. Bachelors marrying per 1000 unmarried in each age group.

Table 2.   England and Wales proportions ever-married, selected years 1901 – 1974.

Males

	1901	1911	1921	1931	1941	1951	1961	1970	1971	1972	1973	1974	1975	1976
16–19	3	2	5	3		7	14	23	26	26	26	24	22	19
20–24	174	143	178	139		229	308	352	369	365	363	352	340	325
25–29	641	508	554	529		647	705	740	743	739	742	739	735	729
30–34	641	728	769	782		810	826	862	862	863	862	861	861	862
35–39	842	814	837	863		867	868	885	889	891	895	896	897	898
40–44	842	852	863	887		892	892	891	892	894	896	899	902	905
45–49	890	873	876	890		902	905	902	900	900	899	900	900	901
50–54	890	886	885	893		914	912	913	913	912	912	911	909	907
55–59	911	902	894	896		923	915	918	918	918	917	916	918	918
60–64	911	900	900	900		922	922	921	922	922	922	921	921	921
65–69	922	912	906	904		917	928	923	923	923	924	925	925	926
70–74	922	920	914	915		916	926	932	930	928	927	926	925	925
75 +	934	932	928	930		922	922	929	937	937	936	935	934	932

Table 2 (continued)

Females

	1901	1911	1921	1931	1941	1951	1961	1970	1971	1972	1973	1974	1975	1976
16–19	19	15	22	22		52	84	99	109	109	112	99	98	89
20–24	274	243	273	258		477	578	591	603	599	594	581	581	574
25–29	660	566	590	594		782	843	866	867	867	867	868	862	857
30–34	660	730	740	751		855	891	920	922	923	924	925	928	930
35–39	815	790	796	794		869	903	927	930	933	936	937	939	940
40–44	815	820	821	819		860	905	923	926	929	932	934	937	940
45–49	864	836	832	832		849	895	921	922	924	926	928	930	933
50–54	864	850	841	841		850	879	913	917	920	923	924	926	927
55–59	883	865	845	843		845	863	901	904	907	910	913	917	920
60–64	883	872	849	845		844	857	880	885	890	895	900	904	907
65–69	889	880	861	842		846	848	866	868	870	874	878	882	887
70–74	889	877	860	844		843	846	859	861	862	864	866	867	869
75+	889	879	868	853		834	840	846	846	848	849	850	852	854

Calculated from OPCS (1977, 1978) Marriage and Divorce Statistics 1975, 1975, Series FM2, 1, 2

1972 was the same as that married in their early forties (40−44) in 1921.

Changes in female nuptiality are more striking, for reasons to be discussed later. In 1901 for example, 86% of women aged 45−49 were married, widowed or divorced—in 1971, 83·2%. By 1951 this percentage rose to 84·9, by 1970 to 92·1. Table 2 shows that the proportion ever-married at age 30−34 in 1951 exceeded that attained at any age in 1931. The 1961 values at age 30−34 exceeded the 1951 proportions at any age, the 1971 values at age 30−34 exceed the 1961 proportions at any age.

A very thorough cohort analysis of marriage since 1900 has been made by Farid (1976). The most recent birth cohort to attain age 50 in these data is that of 1925: as usual in cohort analysis the data which are certain are also obsolete. The results underline recent nuptiality differences between men and women. 906/1 000 men born in 1925 had married by age 50 (gross nuptiality—rather lower than in previous birth cohorts—928 for the 1900 birth cohort). Incomplete data for later cohorts show that the increase in male nuptiality occurs mostly after the 1925 cohort, especially after 1935. But the proportion of women born in 1925 ever-married by age 50 (924) is already much higher than in previous birth cohorts (853 in 1900 birth cohort) and indeed the increase was evident in the 1920 cohort or even earlier. The data emphasize that nuptiality change for men has been primarily a change in timing, while women have experienced both shifts in timing and an increase in the overall level of marriage, which moreover have become apparent earlier in time than have those of men.

Unfortunately, cohort data cannot tell us what is happening at the present time or even what has happened in the recent past, so in order to gauge the import of recent events it is necessary to make estimates and projections, mostly from period data. Period analysis is, in many ways, suitable in the study of marriage and divorce. By contrast with fertility, there is no 'limit' or 'target' at which individuals can aim their ultimate 'performance', adjusting behaviour at one period of their lives to compensate disturbance in an earlier period. Normative social attitudes will obviously affect the propensity to marry and divorce, and cohorts will differ in these as their upbringing differs. But the fact of marriage or of divorce are very much matters of the moment, influenced strongly by

Table 3. Period total first marriage rate (TFMR) and period 'gross nuptiality' (PGN) for selected years, to age 50 (per 1 000 bachelors or spinsters); England and Wales.

	Bachelors			Spinsters		
Year	TFMR	PGN		TFMR	PGN	
1900–1902		880[2]			816[2]	
1911–1915	952·7	898	869[2] (1910–12)	878	843	811[2] (1910–12)
1916–1920		932			845	
1921–1925	1 011·3	925		846	832	
1926–1930		908			828	
1931–1935	926·7	917	899[2] (1930–32)	897	844	826[2] (1930–32)
1936–1940		961	927 (1938)		927	895[2] (1938)
1941–1945		934			915	
1946–1950		949			949	
1951–1955	988·7	935	935[2]	1145	946	945[1]
1956–1960		941			960	
1961–1965	1 021 0 (1961)	938	942[1] (1961)	1 102 (1961)	958	966[1] (1961)
1966		939			957	
1969	980·8	931		1 082	956	
1970	1 016·0	936		1 134	961	
1971	958·7	930		1 082	960	
1972	969·3	936		1 099	967	
1973	901·2	924		1 021	958	
1974	856·5	914		967	951	950*
1975	835·6	907*	912*	942	949*	

Source: calculated from Marriage and Divorce Statistics Series FM2,1 (1974) Table 3.3a, 3.3b, 1.1b pp. 10, 11, 4, 5. PGN single years up to 29, then 5-year age-groups except 1936–1950 all 5-year age groups.
* given in FM2,1 and FM2,2 table 3·8a p. 25
[1] given in Registrar-General's Statistical Review 1961 Volume III Commentary, p. 38 (for age-group 45–49)
[2] given in Hajnal (1947) table 2.

current opportunities and problems. Divorce, especially, is hardly something planned for before marriage.

A simple approach to estimate the current intensity of marriage, rather scorned by British demographers, is to cumulate age-specific marriage rates (for the total, not single, population of each sex) to give the Total First Marriage Rate (TFMR). This gives the total number of first marriages experienced by a synthetic cohort of 1 000 women experiencing the current marriage rates in each age-group (Shryock & Siegel, 1975). This total marriage rate bears the same proportions to the cohort proportions ever-married as does the total fertility rate to completed family size. Its use of the total population by sex as a denominator enables summary rates to be calculated on relatively simple data. It tends to exaggerate proportions ever-married when marriage is becoming more popular or when average age at marriage is falling. With constant proportions 'P' ever-married, a linear fall in age at marriage 'Dm' will give TFMR $= P(1 - Dm)$ (Festy, 1971). So while it indicates the current intensity of marriage, it can reach theoretically impossible values. Total first marriage rates for men (table 3) were 0·953 in 1911−15, 0·927 in 1931−35, 1·021 in 1961 and 1·016 in 1970. Application of the formula above gives 92·8% men ever married by 1961 rates, 91·1% by 1970. Respective figures for spinsters were 0·878, 0·897, 1·102, 1·134.

Two better methods exist for estimating the proportions ever-married at current rates on the basis of probabilities, given the availability of suitable data. First, a simple projection can be made by calculating the survivorship ratios for the unmarried state for a set of birth cohorts over a short period of time, using the proportions single in these cohorts in two successive censuses or population estimates. These survivorship ratios can then be applied to a synthetic cohort as in a life-table (Hajnal, 1947). For example, if the marriage rates between 1961 and 1971 persist then 72 per 1 000 men will still be single at age 45−49 and 46 per 1 000 women. This type of estimate is net of mortality.

Secondly, the effects of current nuptiality can be estimated in a more sophisticated way by converting period age-specific marriage rates into probabilities and applying life-table techniques to a synthetic cohort of individuals single at age 16 to give the survivors single at each successive age. So, for example, period gross nuptiality (ignoring decrements due to mortality) calculations indicate that 942 men per 1 000 and 966 women will marry at least once by age 50 according to 1961 rates, 936 and 961 respectively by 1970 rates (table 3). A simple projection using the proportions single in the cohorts followed from 1969 to 1974 gives 74·7 males per 1 000 single at age 50 and 46·8 per 1 000 women. This simple procedure compares well with OPCS period net nuptiality for 1974 (OPCS, 1977c)—77 per 1 000 single for males, 46 per 1 000 single for females.

These calculations all agree that the continuation of period nuptiality rates at the level observed between 1961 and 1971 will leave less than 8% of men and 5% of women still single at age 49. As always the utility of these estimates depends on the accuracy of the assumptions made. Few formal projections of nuptiality have been made, but, for example, the projection of proportions married made by the Registrar-General on 1959 data for the Robbins Committee (Registrar-General, 1963) considerably underestimated the future intensity of marriage in the younger age-groups. The data available to Hajnal (1947) did not enable him to foresee the progressive rejuvenation of marriage from 1938 onwards, although it was clear by then that there would be a big increase in the proportions 'ever-marrying'.

Since 1964 we have become accustomed to the paradox of a sustained fall of fertility in the midst of nuptiality changes which would normally be expected to increase fertility. But since 1970 nuptiality too has fallen. We only have five years of data, but the magnitude of the change, and its parallel in other European countries make it clear that we are not just witnessing a statistical hiccup.

From 1970 to 1975, mean age at first marriage for bachelors has increased from 23·90 to 24·19 years, for spinsters from 21·79 to 21·97 years. Age-specific first marriage rates have fallen steadily, especially since 1972, in the age groups 15−19 to 30−34, with no corresponding increase at later ages (figure 2). Among bachelors 20−24 the rate has fallen 30·8% from 1970 to 1976 and among 16·19 year olds the fall is 32·7% among bachelors, 30·1% among spinsters. The rise of teenage marriage, one of the most notable demographic developments of the 1950s and 1960s (Rowntree, 1962) has been abruptly halted: teenagers have suffered the sharpest fall in nuptiality of any age-group.

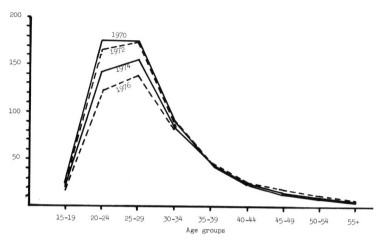

Figure 2.   England and Wales 1970–1976. Bachelors marrying per 1 000 unmarried in each age group. Source EM2, 1, table 3.3a, p. 10; *Population Trends*, 9, 1977, table 23, p. 49; OPCS Monitor FM2 77/4, table 3.

From 1 018·0 per 1 000 bachelors in 1970, TFMR has fallen to 856·55 per 1 000 at the period rates of 1974. Period gross nuptiality for the age-group 45–49 declined from 937 per 1 000 in 1970 to 904 in 1975 for men, and from 959 per 1 000 in 1970 to 947 for women. So now it is male nuptiality which is more volatile, and men who are more likely to remain single all their lives. Is this retreat from marriage just a temporary response to peculiarly depressing economic circumstance or housing difficulties? Is it a return to the old West European marriage pattern'? Or is it the beginning of a new pattern with unique features of its own? These questions must be deferred until the other side of marital change—their breakdown rather than their formation—is examined.

Divorce and remarriage in England and Wales

Remarriages are now a third of all marriages, and the great majority of these remarried persons have been divorced rather than widowed. Marriage cannot usefully be discussed in isolation when divorce rates are so high, because the married state is often re-entered at young ages and divorced people, especially men, will compete with single people for mates, thereby affecting first marriage rates. Furthermore the availability, acceptability and normality of divorce may in itself have some effect upon the propensity to marry for the first time, and on the expectations which young people take with them into marriage (Grebenik & Rowntree, 1963).

Before World War 1, the incidence of divorce in this country was quite negligible. Between 1876 and 1880 there were only 2 301 petitions for dissolution and annulment (almost all the former) of which 1 385 (60%) resulted in decrees absolute. But between 1911–1915 and 1916–1920 there was a three-fold increase in petitions filed (5 167 to 14 768 (286%)). The 1911–1915 rates represent a mere 0·1/1 000 of married population divorcing per year; those of 1916–1920, 0·2/1 000.

It should be made clear that decrees made absolute in a short period do not necessarily refer to petitions filed in that period—and the latter are a more sensitive indicator of temporal trends in dissatisfaction with marriage. The proportions of petitions for divorce resulting in a decree absolute rose from less than 2/3 in World War 1 to more than 3/4 by World War 2, and by 1954–1961 it had risen to 9/10 (Registrar-General, 1963). Another methodological problem was underlined by Chester (1971). He showed that the 'real' duration of marriage of divorced couples—up to separation—is much less than the statistics based upon decrees or even petitions would indicate. A median 2·9 years elapsed between '*de facto*' and '*de jure*' end of the marriage in a provincial sample between 1966 and 1968. As most published rates are based upon decrees, it follows that durations of broken marriages are considerably exaggerated, along with the partners' ages at break-up. As the peak period for divorce is 4–5 years after marriage, it follows that many marriages which fail do so very quickly indeed.

But despite its increased incidence during World War 1, in absolute terms divorce was still a rare phenomenon in the interwar years. Cohort data analysed by Rowntree and Carrier (1958) show that of marriages in 1926, only 0·5% were broken by divorce after 10 years of marriage, 1·9% after 20 years, 4·0% after 30 years (these figures based on petitions). Corresponding figures for the marriages of 1931 and of 1936, although raised successively by about 50% and 30%, still posed no threat to the average marriage —1·01% of the 1936 marriages ended in divorce after 10 years, 5·66% after 20 years, 8·18% after 30 years. Between 1931 and 1935

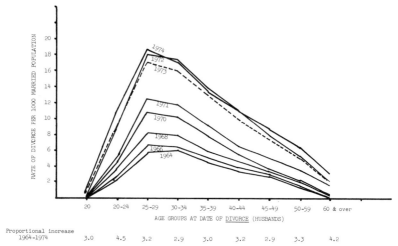

Proportional increase
1964-1974   3.0   4.5   3.2   2.9   3.0   3.2   2.9   3.3   4.2

Figure 3.   England and Wales 1964–1974. Comparison of age-specific
period rates of divorce. FM2 No. 1 (1977), table 4.1a, p. 34.

the level of divorce was equivalent to 0·80 petitions per year filed
per 1 000 married women aged 20–49, and 0·67 decrees absolute
granted per year—about three times the level in World War 1. But
after the passage of the 1937 Matrimonial Causes Act the number
of petitions nearly doubled in one year from 5 903 to 10 233, the
rate of decrees absolute per 1 000 population aged 20–49 increasing
from 0·77 in 1937 to 1·22 in 1939. Some of the increase in rate was
due to a shifting forward in the incidence of divorce by age and
duration of marriage—so that although the proportion of 1941
marriages broken after 10 years was four times that of 1936
marriages, nevertheless the cumulated proportions broken after 20
years was only 34·4% greater and after 30 years only 25% more.

    By 1947 the rate of decrees absolute per 1 000 married women
aged 20–49 was 7 times that of 1940 (8·47/1·15). The disturbed
conditions of World War 2 immediately following a relaxation of
divorce law, had a much more striking effect on divorce than
World War 1. However, this instability of marriage was not sustained after the war: for example only 3·0% of the marriages of
1951 had broken by divorce after 10 years marriage, and 7·4% after
20 years—falls of 26% and 3% respectively compared to the 1941
marriage cohort.

    From the late 1950s onwards we find a rapid rise in divorce to a

much higher level than ever experienced before. In 1960, there were
3·38 decrees absolute per 1 000 married women aged 20–49. By
1969 this was 1/1 000 and 5 years later doubled to 8·1/1 000. Age-
specific rates of divorce, shown in figure 3, indicate that people of
all ages now resort to divorce more frequently than in the past. The
experience of different marriage-cohorts appears to be less important than the particular attitude to divorce experienced by people
from different cohorts at the same point in time. If the incidence of
divorce is most strongly influenced by the legal, economic and
social conditions of the moment, rather than being under the
predominant constraint of a target or ideal informing the attitudes
of each new marriage cohort, then it follows that period methods
of measurement may be more appropriate here than in other areas
of demography. The role of current events and of cohort predispo-
sitions is shown in figure 4: the slight concavity of the cumulative
graph for each cohort (except 1941, 1946) indicating that the effects
of current conditions prevail over the relative fall in duration
specific rates which would otherwise be expected in each cohort.
The latter would give a convex graph approaching an asymptote,
quite unlike those in figure 4.

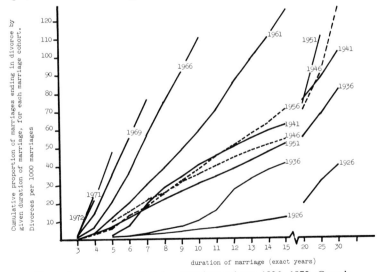

Figure 4. England and Wales. Marriage cohorts 1926–1972. Cumulative divorce rates per 1000 (all ages at marriage). FM2 No. 1 (1977) table
4.4a, p. 44.

Table 4.   Period Total Divorce Rate (TDR) and Period 'Gross Divorciality' (GD) for selected years up to age 50, per 1 000men and women; England and Wales.

	Men		Women		
TDR	GD (married men to age 50, all durations)	TDR	GD (married women, age at marriage <20, 20 years duration)	GD (married women to age 50, all durations)	
1961		81·0*			80·0*
1962					
1963					
1964		118·8	144·7	121·0	
1965		128·5		131·1	
1966		132·4		135·0	
1967		146·6		147·9	
1968		155·5		155·1	
1969	145·1	171·8	152·7	207·1	171·4
1970	166·0	193·5	173·8		191·5
1971	196·9	224·3	207·4	257·6	223·6
1972	302·0	323·7	319·3	369·9	351·2
1973	277·1	307·3	292·9	343·9	304·5
1974	298·1	329·5	313·6	363·7	319·7
1975	320·0	351·9	336·4		341·1
1976	337·4		354·5		

Sources: Calculated from:
Marriage and Divorce Statistics 1974 Series FM2, 1, FM2,2. table 1·1, 4·1a, 4·3c.
Monitor pp. 77/3 New Population Estimates for England and Wales mid 1971 to
mid 1976. tables 1·6.
Monitor FM2 77/3 Divorces 1975 and 1976.
Registrar-General's Statistical Review 1969 Part II table P.2 p. 68.

*'net divorciality', given in Schoen and Nelson (1974).

The current intensity of divorce is such that the period total divorce rate (that is, the cumulated age-specific probability of divorce per 1 000 women in each group to age 49) rose from 90·5/1 000 in 1960 to 313·6 in 1974. That is, in 1974 of 1 000 married women experiencing the current divorce rates, 300 would end their marriage in divorce by age 49 (table 4). Of course there are many problems in the interpretation of such figures—and they underline certain difficulties in the study of the life of marriages. Marriages can begin their lives at any age over 16 and their survival chances depend upon the ages of both partners and in other personal attributes. Wives married at less than age 20 were more than 4 times more likely to divorce after 10 years marriage than where the wife married at age 35–39. Their survival chances also decline with duration—the peak rate being in the fourth completed year almost regardless of age at marriage. Marriages may be destroyed by divorce, and also by death. Total marriages rates, as well as having the built-in volatility associated with all summed period rates, also ignore the decrements of death—avoided in the most part by considering marriages up to age 49 only.

The mean duration of marriages ended by divorce has declined only slightly—from 12·9 years in 1964 to 12·3 years in 1970. After that, the mean duration increased to 13·6 but this was due to the backlog of older broken marriages awaiting disposal by the new Divorce Law Reform Act—by 1974 it was down to 13·0 years. There is obviously an underlying trend for marriages to end sooner but the mean age at divorce has also fallen because of the fall in the age at marriage and because working class people who marry earlier, now resort to divorce much more than in the past (Gibson, 1974). This is so partly because of legal changes affecting Legal Aid (Registrar-General, 1963). Mean age at divorce fell from 39·1 in 1964 to 37·6 in 1973 for husbands and from 36·3 in 1974 to 34·8 in 1970 for wives.

Can the predictions inherent in the period rates be confirmed by reference to other sources of data? One simple alternative method is to compare the proportion divorced by given duration of marriage between two cohorts and apply this ratio to the proportion divorced in the earlier cohort and the longer durations of marriage which the younger cohort has not yet experienced. For example, the 1970 cohort at 6 years duration of marriage had experienced 4·77 times the divorces of the 1951 cohort at the same duration. If this applies throughout the period then this implies 352·0/1 000 divorced by 20 years duration of marriage (4·77 × 73·8). This is based on the 1951 marriages up to 1971, excluding the great increase, especially in older marriages, following the 1969 Act (which did not become effective until 1 January 1971).

The most complete way of describing the life and death of marriages is to construct survival tables on the life-table principle indicating decrements due to divorce and to death, from which average duration of marriage and other statistics can be calculated (Shryock & Siegel, 1975; Maison, 1974). Schoen and Nelson (1974) have prepared multiple decrement and increment tables using data from the United States and England and Wales, incorporating marriage, death, divorce and remarriage. They showed for England and Wales that the average life of a marriage according to 1961 data was 38·4 years, and the corresponding probability that a marriage would end in divorce was 0·081 (males) and 0·080 (females). This corresponds quite well with the period Total Divorce Rate for 1961 0·0895 up to age 49. I have not attempted to apply their techniques to more recent English marriages. But a single-decrement marriage table, based upon marriage breakdown probabilities from divorce only (derived, in a fashion analogous to gross nuptiality, from duration-specific divorce rates) suggests that 264/1 000 marriages of women aged up to 20 years at marriage will have ended in divorce by the 20th completed year of marriage (that is, between ages 40−44 at 1974 rates, compared to 145 at 1964 rates). This is quite similar to the estimates made by other means: results of the same procedure applied to age-specific rates (all durations) up to age 49 are given in table 4. Estimates made in different ways suggest that 1 in 10 marriages will end in divorce according to 1961 period divorce rates, while divorce will end at least 1 in 3 marriages according to period rates prevailing in 1974. These figures ignore the effects of mortality. Note that they include divorces of remarriages as well as first marriages although the former are, so far, a relatively minor component. There is some evidence that remarriages, especially for both partners, are more prone to end in divorce than are first marriages.

Remarriages
    The demographic consequences of high divorce rates are considerable. By 1971 it has been estimated (DHSS Report of the Committee in One-Parent Families, 1974) that there were 520 000 fatherless one-parent families with dependent children in Great Britain. Of these, 190 000 or 37% resulted from separation of the parents, 120 000 or 23% were the result of divorce. However, the recent popularity of divorce has not generated a large *number* of unmarried but divorced people in the population, although the

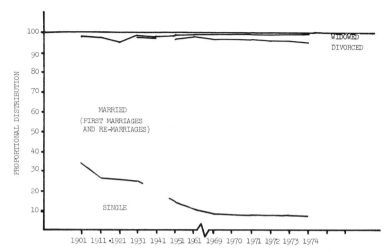

Figure 5.   England and Wales 1901–1974. Marital status of population
by age. Women 30–34. FM2 No. 1, table 1.1b, p. 5.

proportion has greatly increased—from 1/1 000 women in 1931 to
17·1/1 000 in 1974. As figure 5 shows, the number relative to the
rest of the population is still tiny, reaching a maximum of 38/1 000
among all women aged 30–39 and less than 80/1 000 married
women in the peak age group 35–39 in 1976 (see Leete, 1977b).
Divorced people, especially men, frequently remarry. Remarriage
rates increased slightly up to 1972 and have not shared the recent
precipitous fall in nuptiality. Since then first marriages have
become a progressively smaller sector of the marriage scene as high
divorce rates open up a new marriage market, only a few years after
the peak years for first marriages. In 1970 first marriages were
818/1 000; by 1974, partly as a result of the Divorce Reform Act
1969, they were down to 707/1 000 and by 1976 to 680/1 000
marriages. Of the 321/1 000 remarriages in 1976, 176 (54·8%) were
between one previously single and one previously married person,
143 (44·5%) were remarriages for both. Since 1946–50 remarriages
involving divorced persons have outnumbered those involving
widowed persons. The ratio is now 9:1 in 'single remarriages' and
4:1 in 'double remarriages' (89·7%:10·3%, 63·6%:16·9%. FM2
table 3.2d, Monitor FM2 77/4 table 2). In absolute terms, the
number of first marriages has been falling fast—from 302 000 to

274 000 between 1974 and 1976, while over the same period the number of remarriages increased 28·5% from 112 717 to 144 979. Even by 1961 rates, Schoen and Nelson (1974) estimated that 12% ever-married men would marry more than once, and a projection made in the early 1970s for the Finer Committee estimated that 20% of ever-married men aged 65 in the year 2001 would have married more than once.

Comparisons with other western countries: marriage

The other industrial nations of the free world—the United States, Canada, Australia and New Zealand—have, in general, shared these trends. In most countries age at first marriage has declined from 28−29 for bachelors and 24−25 for spinsters at the turn of the century, to 24−25 for men and 22−23 for women in the early 1970s. Proportions ever-married by age 50 have generally increased, especially among women and, since the late 1960s, all have experienced a check to nuptiality. The trends are shared both by nations with initially high age at marriage and low nuptiality (Ireland, Sweden) by those with low age at marriage and high nuptiality (the United States) and even, at least among women, in semi-industrialized countries such as Greece. A general review up to 1960 has been given by Ryder (1963) and recent trends in Europe are described by Festy and Prioux (1975).

Festy (1973) conveniently assembled cohort data showing the advance of nuptiality in the United States, Canada, Australia and New Zealand. For example, mean age at marriage for bachelors in the 1901−1905 birth cohort was respectively 28·1, 27·0, 28·3 and 28·0 in these countries. But in the birth cohorts of 1936−1940 these means had fallen to 24·8, 23·7, 25·6 and 25·3 years. Between these same cohorts, proportions ever-married by age 50 rose from 98, 89, 88 and 90% to 92, 94, 94 and 95% (projected). Even in 1930 the proportions single at age 45−49 in these countries were lower than in Europe (14% of men, 10% of women in the USA; 12% of men, 9% of women in Canada). As these figures show, female nuptiality benefited from the excess of men caused by the male emigration which so weakened European womens' chances of marriage. The sex ratios were notably more favourable than in Europe (Glass, 1976 and Festy & Prioux, 1975). Furthermore these countries were spared most of the burden of male mortality suffered in Europe after the two World Wars (Barnett, 1972 and Winter, 1976). By 1970 their proportions single were the lowest of any country in the West, with low age at marriage to match; a median 20·3 for American spinsters in 1960, for example.

Figure 6 shows the general rise in nuptiality in Europe since the war, through the summary measure of total first marriage rate. These and other data show some interesting deviations from the general trend. In France, singulate mean age at marriage (see Hajnal, 1953) was already much lower than that of its neighbours even at the beginning of the 19th century (van de Walle, 1972) and declined steadily from then on—in advance of the rest of Europe but in line with its own precocious fall in fertility. The intensity of French nuptiality accelerated rather erratically after the war. After the postwar boom it fell further in the 1950s than most other European countries, especially in 1956 through the effects, according to French demographers (Maison & Millet, 1974 and Pressat, 1962) of the Algerian conflict. Between 1964 and 1970, age specific marriage rates reached high levels especially in the age-groups 20–22, then subsequently declining (INED, 1977). Nuptiality, both in France and in West Germany, declines before any fall is apparent in England and Wales. TFMR peaked in France in 1965 (for men) and in Germany in 1967–68. In Western Europe, Switzerland is perhaps the most extreme example of early decline. The intensity of nuptiality (TFMR) began to fall from 1962 (953 for men, 943 for women), averaged 877 for bachelors and 891 for spinsters between 1962 and 1970, and fell very sharply after 1970; TFMR for the next five years averaged only 714 for men and 752 for women—by 1975 it did not greatly exceed 600. As in the rest of Europe, male nuptiality has fallen far more than female, although nuptiality among the neutral Swiss was very similar for each sex until 1966. Labour immigration may be partly responsible for the subsequent divergence (Mouvement de la Population en Suisse, 1975). Other countries, such as Holland, have shown consistently higher levels of nuptiality throughout this period, with age-specific rates for the under-24s peaking as late as 1970 or even 1974 for teenage girls (see *Statistical Yearbook of the Netherlands*, 1976). This late fall from high nuptiality may perhaps be attributed to the demographic warfare between the two ethnic and religious groups in Holland. Italy, by contrast, has shown consistently lower nuptiality than the West

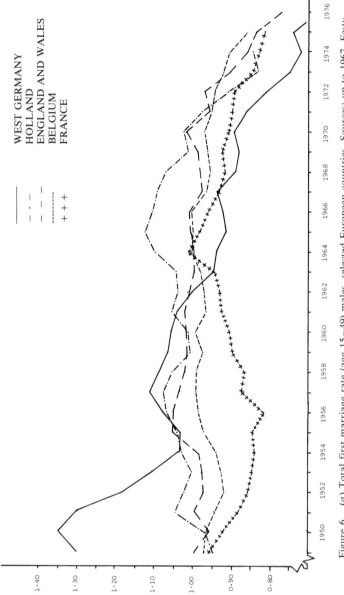

Figure 6. (*a*) Total first marriage rate (age 15–49) males, selected European countries. Sources: up to 1967, Festy (1971) then calculated from vital registration statistics of each country. Also Lery, A. (1975) Données de démographie générale. Nuptialité 1931–73, Paris, INSEE.

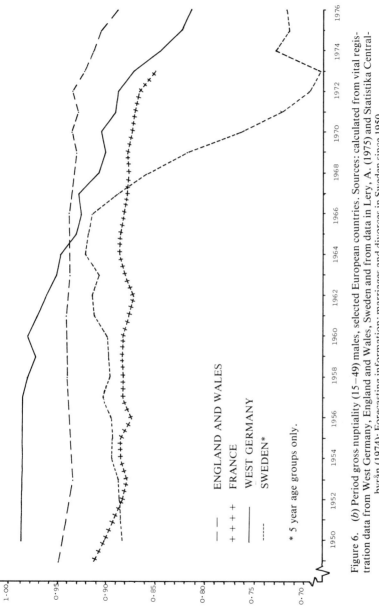

Figure 6. (b) Period gross nuptiality (15–49) males, selected European countries. Sources: calculated from vital registration data from West Germany, England and Wales, Sweden and from data in Lery, A. (1975) and Statistika Centralbyrån (1974): Forecasting information: marriages and divorces in Sweden since 1950.

ENGLAND AND WALES

FRANCE

WEST GERMANY

SWEDEN*

* 5 year age groups only.

European average. Earlier this century, the inhabitants of Southern Ireland, especially men, married very late, if at all, so that the population included a uniquely high proportion of elderly bachelors. In contrast to Scandinavia, the unmarried did not usually console themselves with any permanent form of unmarried cohabitation. But in the last few decades, marriage has become much more popular and the average age is much closer to the European average (for a cohort study see Brahimi, 1978) although the intensity of marriage is still considerably lower than in England and Wales. In 1974, age-specific marriage rates in England and Wales were three times those of Southern Ireland in the 15–19 age group, 1½ times the Irish figure in the 20–24 age-group (see *Southern Ireland Report on Vital Statistics*, 1974). This change has come about partly in response to the moderation of excess female emigration from Ireland, partly through recent economic expansion.

In most of Europe, the nuptiality advantage held by men before the war has passed to women, whose nuptiality has since accelerated faster and then stayed more stable in the recent decline. This is not so in West Germany, nor in Italy. In the former, the imbalance of the marriage market in favour of men was preserved by the heavy male mortality in World War 2 as well as in World War 1. This situation endured until postwar birth cohorts reached marriageable age in recent years. Switzerland was the only non-combatant country which did not also experience heavy male emigration, so there the nuptiality of the sexes has evolved more in parallel.

Throughout this period, American nuptiality has been more intense than in Europe. But the fall in the mean age at marriage was arrested and reversed in the late 1960s, just like everywhere else. For example, Schoen and Nelson (1974) give period net nuptiality for California in 1960 as 945 (England and Wales 1961, 933) but by 1969 it had fallen to 928. Glick and Norton (1973) attribute this fall to higher college attendance and to the removal of young men for service in the Vietnam War (which is also thought to have pushed up divorce rates). But similar changes occurred at the same time in Europe, so a more general explanation is called for.

The 'Swedish marriage pattern'
Since the late 1960s marriage patterns in Scandinavia, especially

in Sweden and Denmark, have developed unique features of their own which warrant special consideration. These changes may appear to mark a return to the old West European marriage pattern, but in fact the resemblance is only superficial. Sweden has always been a demographic oddity in Europe, and so to some extent have the rest of Scandinavia and Iceland. The following data come mostly from Prioux-Marchal (1974), Prioux (1977), and the *Statistical Abstract of Iceland* (1974).

For example, among the birth cohort of 1881–1885, 16% of Swedish men and 23% of women were still single at 50 (that is in 1931–35). But, as in the rest of Europe, proportions single fell from the birth cohorts of 1901–1905, rapidly for women, more slowly for men (as the sex ratio declined with the end of emigration) to reach 13 and 6% respectively for the cohorts born between 1920 and 1930 (14 and 8% in 1970). These are still rather high levels, especially for males. This nuptiality transition was completed earlier than in the rest of Europe; 1965 was the peak year both for Crude and Total marriage rates. Age at first marriage followed suit, falling from a remarkable peak of 29·7 for men and 27·2 for women in the cohorts 1901–1905, to typical recent values of 25 and 23 respectively in the birth cohorts of 1941–1945. Between 1950 and 1964 the total first marriage rate for both sexes remained between 0·9 and 1·0. Swedish nuptiality did not accelerate in the postwar periods: most of the change from the old pattern was accomplished before the war.

But after 1964, period nuptiality shows an extraordinary and so far uniquely strong decline, such that the total first marriage rate fell from 0·958 (men) and 0·944 (women) in 1964, to only 0·51 (men) and 0·56 (women) in 1973. Naturally this has been accompanied by a sharp rise in the proportion single. Birth cohorts of 1941–45 are projected to comprise 14% women and 21% men never-married by age 50. At 1972 rates, the later birth cohort of 1949–1950 would comprise 42·5% never-married men and 36% never-married women at this age. Such rates for women would be without precedent except for those Swiss cantons which restricted the marriage of the poor by law in the 19th century, and by the extraordinarily high rate of (non-celibate) spinsterhood in historical Icelandic populations (Tomasson, 1977). However, since 1973 marriage rates have risen somewhat (Prioux, 1977) and the TFMR has stabilized at 0·65 in 1974 and 1975. The intensity of remarriage has fallen too, though not as steeply as first marriage rates, so they have risen slightly as a proportion of all marriages from 9·8% in 1966 to 13·3% in 1972, despite a fall since 1965 of 57% in the remarriages of widowers and 75% of those of divorced men.

Although fertility has fallen since 1965, it has not fallen in line with marital changes because illegitimate fertility has to some extent—not completely—replaced it. Historically, Sweden has always had high illegitimacy rates (16% in 1926–30) due partly to different customs relating to cohabitation during betrothal, and to a relatively casual attitude to marriage. The rate fell to 9·9% in 1951–1955, as was general in Europe, from 19th century levels, (Shorter *et al.*, 1971), but then doubled from 1961–1965 (12·8%) to 31·4% in 1974—by far the highest in Western Europe except for Iceland (34·0% in 1974). Marriage is ceasing to be the predominant setting for fertility. Premarital but legitimate conceptions have scarcely increased and cohabiting couples are tending more and more to have children before marriage, although they may marry afterwards as was the custom in medieval Europe and elsewhere (Laslett, 1969). Moreover, the marriages which are formed are progressively less stable. Between 1941–45 and 1961–65, the total divorce rate increased gradually from 108 to 166/1 000, then to 190 in 1966 and 281 in 1972. Law reform in 1973 made divorce even easier than before; in 1974 TDR rose to an astonishing 522, falling slightly to 502 in 1975.

Other Scandinavian countries have followed this example although in a less extreme way (Prioux, 1977). For Sweden, Norway, Finland and Denmark mean age at marriage for women in the 1940–41 birth cohort was 23·3, 22·7, 23·3 and 22·5 years respectively. Since 1965 Denmark, and since 1967 Norway and Finland, have all shared in the decline of nuptiality but especially Denmark.

In 1973, Danish TFMR rose slighlty in line with Sweden's but the higher rates of Finland and Norway continued to fall, the decline being strongest at younger ages. Although large numbers of people continue to cohabit without marriage in Iceland, as they have in the past, age-specific marriage rates rose to a peak for the under thirties in 1966–70 and have since fallen to the levels of the early 1960s. Mean age at marriage reached a low value in 1973 for bachelors

(24·6 years) and in 1972 for spinsters (22·8 years)—these have
since risen to 25·0 and 23·0 respectively in 1974. Denmark, too,
shows similar fertility changes to Sweden. In 1974, 18% of all
births were illegitimate—twice the proportion in England and
Wales—compared to 10·2% in 1966 and 6–8% in 1951–55. But
Norway and Finland do not seem to be following the same
example. Their illegitimacy rates are only 6·7% in 1972 (Finland)
(4·8% in 1966) and 9·33 in 1974 (4·9 in 1966) (Norway). Neither do
changes in divorce quite follow the Swedish pattern. In 1974 TDR
was 358/1 000 in Denmark (186 in 1966), 231 in Finland (145 in
1966) and 190 in Norway (106 in 1966).

Demographers need to learn more about premarital cohabitation
if it is becoming a partial substitute or a usual preliminary to
formal marriage. A survey mounted in 1974 in Denmark
(Andersen, 1976, quoted in Roussel, 1977) gives us some insights
into the new situation. In the population 20–29 years old, a maximum of 41% were living together without marriage and only 32%
were married. Beyond age 23 only a tiny proportion (less than 5%)
still lived with their parents. Even 23% of 18 year old girls lived
with their boyfriends. Altogether about 12% of all couples lived
together without being married, 60% of these being below 30 years
of age. The proportion of unmarried females aged 20–24 increased
from 44% in 1970 to 59% in 1975. The rate of illegitimate births
has shot up since 1970 despite a most liberal abortion law, but there
has still been a particular fall in the ASFR in ages 20–22.

When asked why they lived together (instead of marrying), 4%
of bachelors stated that they intended to marry soon, 36% were
having 'a trial marriage'. But 25% insisted that marriage formali-
ties were 'pointless' and another 8% never had marriage in mind at
all. After 5 years of more of cohabitation, 48% still intended to
marry, compared to 82% of 1 years' duration (average 69%). So
for about half of these couples marriage is being delayed for several
years; in others formal marriage may never take place at all. The
rate of break-up of these couples is not known, but married women
report an average period of premarital cohabitation of 1·2 years,
tending to marry when the first child is born.

Is there any evidence that England and Wales might follow the
same pattern? Certainly divorce is very high—among the highest
rates in Europe. Certainly illegitimacy is rising as a proportion of

births—but it is not rising fast and it is low compared to many other European countries. And far fewer brides are pregnant at marriage than even a few years ago (Leete, 1977a). Only 9% of all births were illegitimate in 1976, although illegitimate births made up 29% of all fertility of mothers up to age 20 (Pearce & Farid, 1977). Certainly nuptiality has fallen, but to nowhere near the Swedish levels. And premarital cohabitation? A survey of recent marriages (1972–1973) in Reading, Berkshire (see Coleman, 1977a) showed that 7·5% couples had moved to live together before marriage. (13·1% gave the same address on their marriage certificates but some of these were the addresses of parents and future parents-in-law.) These couples came predominantly from social classes I and II and from the higher educational levels. However, among remarriages, who numbered 30% of the sample, 45% lived together before marriage. And these couples, interestingly enough, were more evenly distributed along the class scale and by educational level. So altogether 17·9% of the couples appeared to have lived together before marriage—I have no information on how long. Neither do I know of data relating to cohabitation which does not end in marriage.

Circumstances do not seem right for the Swedish pattern to be adopted in Britain. Except for the collapse of nuptiality in Switzerland since 1970, few components of this pattern are found together outside Scandinavia. The nuptiality history of some Scandinavian countries—especially Sweden and Iceland—is unique in Europe in its combination of a high proportion of formally illegitimate children compared to Ireland, which combined a high proportion of unmarried people with low levels of cohabitation and illegitimacy. Cohabitation on a wide scale in modern countries, especially if children are to be born outside marriage, is probably a response to a basic high standard and high cost of living, easy availability of housing, and laws and taxes which only weakly distinguish between unmarried and married couples and their children, in an indulgent moral climate of opinion. These conditions are not fulfilled in Britain. But a recent survey shows that the frequency of cohabitation in France seems to be high compared to neighbouring countries. A survey of marriages conducted in 1977 (apparently both first and remarriages, but restricted to persons aged 18–29) showed that the proportion who had lived together before marriage rose from 17% of the 1968–69 cohort to 26% in the 1972–73 cohort (compare the Reading 1972–73 value of 18% for all ages at marriage) to 44% of the 1976–77 cohort (Roussel, 1978).

Comparisons with other Western countries: divorce

Most Western countries have experienced changes in nuptiality more or less in step, and from similar base levels. Divorce is different. Base levels vary considerably between different countries. In Ireland, divorce is still non-existent; in Italy and Spain, rather low. In Scandinavia and North America, divorce eventually affects a high proportion of marriages; most European countries are somewhere in the middle. To some extent, the history of divorce change is the history of its legal status. Most countries have laws to protect the family and to impede divorce. For example, until the Matrimonial Causes Act, 1857 civil divorce required a private Act of Parliament, and the grounds for divorce were not widened beyond adultery until the Matrimonial Causes Act (the 'Herbert Act') of 1937. Legal aid to petitioners whose poverty had previously restricted their access to the divorce courts (Rowntree & Carrier, 1958) was not widely available until the Legal Aid and Advice Act, 1947 and again in the Legal Aid Act, 1960 (see Registrar-General, 1963). And recently the Divorce Reform Act, 1969 which substituted 'irremediable breakdown' after three years' marriage as the sole cause for dissolution instead of 'matrimonial offence', and which permitted divorce by consent after two years' separation, precipitated a flood of divorces of long-dead marriages.

Most European countries have reformed their divorce legislation since 1969 (reviewed in Festy & Prioux, 1975). But much of the great increase in the incidence of divorce in the late 1960s took place before these laws were changed and must reflect deep changes in society in general. The graphs in figure 7 (taken from Festy and Prioux, 1975) illustrate a number of points. (1) Not surprisingly, the incidence of divorce at any given time varies by more than two-fold between different countries—more than any other demographic parameter except abortion. France, Italy, Belgium, Holland, Switzerland and Norway show the lowest rates, as might be expected from the relatively restrictive nature of their divorce legislation.

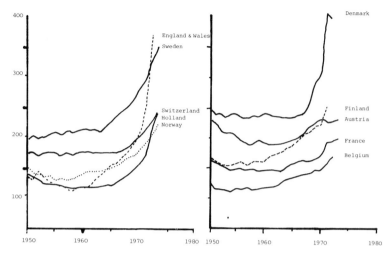

Figure 7. Period total divorce rate per 1 000 marriages 1950–1973, selected West European and Scandinavian countries. Source Festy and Prioux (1975).

(2) Changes in the intensity of divorce occur at about the same time in different countries—in general a fall from high wartime and postwar levels to the 1950s in all but the neutral countries, followed by stability during the 1950s. Projections made then showed that between 6·5% (Belgium) and 18·5% (Denmark) of marriages would end in divorce (England and Wales, 7%; Holland, 7%, France, 9·5%). In all countries divorce then increases rapidly from the 1960s onwards, so far without interruption. Divorce rates specific for marriage duration show that failed marriages often end very quickly in all countries; in the 1950s for example, all peak at between 4 and 6 years duration except Germany and Austria where the mode was three years. Legal restrictions may prevent it from being even earlier, and Chester's (1971) caveat obviously applies here. Festy and Prioux (1975) quote a French sample showing that 2·3 years elapse between the death of the marriage by separation and the final divorce.

High divorce rates in the United States have for long been a source of public interest and amusement in Europe. Before World War 2, divorce rates were about three times higher than English levels; 10/1 000 married women aged 14–44 in 1921–1923,

13/1 000 in 1936−1938 (Glick & Norton, 1973). As in other bellige-
rent countries divorce rates doubled by the end of World War 2
(24/1 000 in 1945−47) and then fell once more by the mid-1950s.
But since then divorce has been rising rapidly from 16/1 000 in
1960−1962 to 26/1 000 in 1969−71. Schoen and Nelson's multiple
decrement and increment tables show that by 1960 period data
259/1 000 marriages would end in divorce (for women, 264 for
men), compared to 81 and 80 in England and Wales, 1961. The
expectation of life of an American marriage in that year was 30·8
years, compared to 38·4 years in England and Wales in 1961. These
divorce and remarriage rates would give 1·28 marriages per person
(1·36 per person marrying). In life-table calculations on 1965 data,
quoted in Shryock and Siegel (1975), 300/1 000 marriages where
the bride is aged 20−24 end in divorce, 442 where the bride is aged
15−20. Projections made for the 1940−1944 birth cohort suggest
that between 25 and 29% of all marriages will end in divorce,
compared to 21−23% for the 1930−1934 birth cohort, 18−19% for
the 1920−24 birth cohort and 14−15% for the 1910−1914 cohort
(Glick & Norton, 1973). Customs vary considerably between
American states. If California is the vanguard of American social
change then divorce rates can be expected to rise even further. In
1960, Californian marriages already had a probability of 0·328 of
ending in divorce, with a high rate of remarriage and re-divorce—
the average person marrying experiencing 1·46 marriages and 0·479
divorces. The expectation of life of a marriage was 28·6 years. By
1969 rates, 400/1 000 marriages would end in divorce and the
average person marrying would enjoy 1·55 marriages and 0·619
divorces. Californian rates were in excess of those of Sweden at
that time.

Causes of change in patterns of marriage and divorce

In the short run, period marriage rates are quite volatile and it is
often possible to link their fluctuations with fluctuations in the
economy. Thomas (1927) linked American nuptiality change with
the business cycle and Glass (1938) showed a relationship between
deviations of real wages and nuptiality from their respective
moving averages in England and Wales between 1954 and 1937. But
the amplitude was low despite a correlation of 0·6, and getting less
towards the end of the period. However, the relationship can still

be detected in more modern marriages: for the USA 1920–1957 (Kirk, 1960, in Shryock & Siegel, 1975, p. 568) and for Britain in the 1960s (Silver, 1966). The PIC marriage survey of 1959–60 (Grebenik & Rowntree, 1963) did show that economic prospects and housing worries had some effect of the timing of marriage, but it was much less than expected: possibly because the question was asked too late in the cycle of family formation after engagement.

Marriage rates and ages at marriage by sex can be strongly affected by an unbalanced sex ratio. This puts the more numerous sex in a 'marriage squeeze' forcing it to marry into unfashionable age-groups or to remain single. Given men's preference for younger women, past variations in fertility will automatically put the marriage market out of the equilibrium (Henry, 1975; Akers, 1967; Muhsam, 1974). Through selective male emigration and the excess male mortality of World War 1 (and World War 2 in some countries) women were in such a squeeze in the first few decades of this century, in most European countries. These effects have now disappeared and the fall in mortality ensures that males are the majority sex until about age 50 (table 5). The position is now reversed so that male nuptiality is now more volatile, and at a lower level, than that of women, hence the more rapid change in female than in male nuptiality since the 1930s. The recent change in the age-difference at marriage is due to men being obliged to marry into age-groups of women that were previously less fashionable (table 6). A minor contribution to the squeeze on men will have been made by the initially unbalanced sex ratio of Commonwealth immigrants (see Immigrant Statistics Unit, 1978), but this is now normalizing and the progressively bigger birth cohorts now moving into peak marriage-ages may (through differential age at marriage) restore a more balanced system.

These are essentially short-term matters. The really interesting problem is the radical change which occurred to the European marriage pattern over the last 40 years, and the threat to it posed by the fall of nuptiality in the last few years. One point of view is that the fall in the mean age at marriage and the increase in nuptiality since the last century is the final act of the demographic transition. The West European marriage pattern may have been an essential pre-condition for the industrial and agricultural revolution which, by radically improving material standards of living, caused

Table 5.   Sex ratio males/1 000 females in given age-groups; England and Wales.

	All persons													
	1901	1911	1921	1931	1951	1961	1969	1970	1971	1972	1973	1974	1975	1976
16–19	974	981	966	968	1 017	1 030	1 040	1 049	1 056	1 063	1 061	1 058	1 054	1 055
20–24	893	898	850	946	1 003	1 026	1 027	1 024	1 026	1 029	1 033	1 035	1 045	1 055
25–29	888	897	827	943	996	1 041	1 033	1 031	1 029	1 027	1 024	1 027	1 026	1 023
30–34	909	916	843	884	980	1 020	1 042	1 040	1 041	1 037	1 035	1 037	1 034	1 031
35–39	931	933	865	844	971	1 001	1 022	1 026	1 030	1 034	1 036	1 038	1 041	1 035
40–44	942	929	888	857	978	981	1 000	1 001	1 002	1 008	1 012	1 020	1 024	1 027
45–49	935	927	934	868	957	958	974	974	982	988	993	995	995	997
	Single persons only													
Males 20–29/ Females 16–24	682	773	682	627	952	822	831	850	860	863	858	844	846	847
20–24	1 017	1 017	963	1 098	1 481	1 680	1 628	1 624	1 632	1 631	1 621	1 603	1 646	1 673
25–29	938	1 017	900	1 092	1 612	1 957	1 994	1 995	1 995	2 011	1 991	2 028	1 974	1 936
30–34	960	924	751	774	1 284	1 633	1 767	1 790	1 835	1 849	1 876	1 934	2 000	2 048
35–39	796	825	691	561	982	1 358	1 604	1 607	1 621	1 664	1 684	1 700	1 757	1 773
40–44	805	767	677	536	756	1 107	1 385	1 414	1 459	1 506	1 539	1 563	1 588	1 624
45–49	757	715	693	567	621	871	1 163	1 202	1 250	1 295	1 342	1 390	1 421	1 475
16–19	990	991	983	1 005	1 065	1 109	1 122	1 138	1 155	1 162	1 164	1 145	1 143	1 136

Source: Marriage and Divorce Statistics 1974, 1975 Series FM2, 1, 2 Table 1·1a.

Table 6. Age-distribution of wives per 10 000 husbands aged 24, selected years; England and Wales.

Year	16	17	18	19	20	21	22	23	24	25–29	30–34	35–39	40–44
1921*	5	42	202	508	820	1409	1433	1539	1502	2312	200	21	2
1926*	9	44	213	471	775	1374	1530	1605	1513	2257	184	20	3
1931	16	89	249	503	841	1374	1535	1587	1389	2178	200	28	3
1936	22	82	233	492	851	1473	1610	1569	1331	2122	184	23	3
1946	25	127	410	774	1124	1553	1535	1388	1150	1699	174	29	5
1951	26	126	441	955	1386	1759	1530	1225	943	1393	168	33	7
1956	35	193	578	1091	1501	1891	1445	1153	815	1114	141	21	6
1956*	68	260	690	1198	1494	1863	1524	1122	758	921	85	10	3
1961	67	256	677	1177	1469	1832	1506	1119	766	983	113	25	7
1964	63	253	590	1181	1675	1927	1497	1020	697	951	108	29	6
1966	46	177	591	1287	1527	1917	1604	1124	711	879	107	21	5
1968	56	168	468	945	1488	2183	1576	1191	813	963	117	25	6
1970	56	163	545	954	1316	1689	1699	1514	815	1073	136	30	8
1971	58	189	564	947	1270	1639	1595	1396	1059	1112	142	29	7
1972	64	201	619	952	1217	1518	1518	1364	971	1360	165	38	8
1973	66	209	635	979	1257	1503	1498	1264	912	1433	180	49	12
1973*	71	223	670	1045	1350	1603	1576	1305	910	1159	71	15	1
1974	62	233	661	999	1285	1495	1432	1275	903	1394	199	48	12
1974*	63	247	699	1066	1378	1602	1512	1316	900	1122	82	9	2

*Bachelor/spinster marriages.

Source: Registrar-General's Statistical Review Part II Population Table I,J Marriage and Divorce Statistics Series FM2 table 3·7 p. 22.

mortality to fall (Spengler, 1972). A subsequent fall in fertility was necessary in order to preserve the advance made in family and in national prosperity, and it was made possible through the liberating effects of wider education and less rigid moral attitudes (Banks, 1954). Steady Victorian economic growth did not radically reduce marriage because fertility did not begin to fall until the 1870s and where fertility had fallen earlier, as in France, age at first marriage and then proportions single fell with it (van de Walle, 1972). Furthermore, Victorian economic growth averaged about 1½% per annum, while postwar growth has averaged about 3½% (Deane & Cole, 1969). The decline in British fertility from 1870, completed by 1930, made it finally clear that births could be contained within marriage by birth control, without the need to defer weddings. This weaker association between marriage and fertility should, in turn, lessen the connection between nuptiality and economic fluctuations (Glass, 1938). As delayed marriage had become, by the 1930s, an unnecessary form of delayed gratification, age at marriage and proportions single fell to more natural levels. This can only have been helped by the way in which the 20th century European family is better insulated by social welfare against low wages and unemployment. As each individual's peers were married off faster, the norm of marriages will have fallen and maybe seeded a general increase in the popularity of marriage. Fear of being 'left on the shelf' strikes at earlier and earlier ages (Glass, 1976; Rayner, 1973) so changes in age at marriage, although theoretically separate from proportions marrying, may in practice have a direct effect upon them.

Prosperity also presses on marriage rates by lowering the age of sexual maturity. Along with secular increases in height and weight, median age at menarche has fallen, by about 0·3 years per decade, in Britain and in all other industrial countries. Age at menarche has fallen from about 15 years in 1900 to about 13 in 1970 (Tanner, 1973), although in England and Norway at least, the trend seems to have stopped. Malthus' remark seems still to be true, that 'towards the extinction of the passion between the sexes, no observable progress has hitherto been made'. Sexual activity now begins correspondingly earlier (Schofield, 1965) and, it seems reasonable to assume, a feeling for permanent sexual relationships in marriage. Certainly, for marriage cohorts 1920–1960, the mean age at which future spouses first meet has fallen as well as the age at marriage, although the time between meeting and marriage has also shortened somewhat—for husbands aged 30 or less, from 2·99 years in 1920–29 cohorts to 3·23 years in those marrying between 1950 and 1960 (Coleman, 1977b).

Nuptiality decline in the last few years may confound these remarks. But at least some of the fall is due to the way it is measured—age-specific rates summing to a TFMR of more than one per person cannot be sustained and can only occur during an unstable transitional phase when marriage age is falling and the proportions marrying are already high. Period nuptiality rates in the late 1950s and 60s were inflated for the same reason (Farid, 1976). When the situation stabilizes, TFMR must fall even if there is no fall in lifetime probability of marrying. But many marriages have undoubtedly been posponed since the 1960s: and if marriage is postponed too long, it may never take place. It seems to me that the reason lies in a conventional economic relationship with nuptiality. Since the late 1960s, although economic growth has continued at a lower level, Western countries have experienced accelerating levels both of unemployment and of inflation—previously thought to be an impossible combination. Since the war the Western economies have become unusually closely synchronized and the simultaneous boom in 1971–72 led quickly to a world-wide commodity price inflation in 1973, exacerbated by the oil crisis (see OECD statistics in *The Economist* 14–20 January 1978.) The subsequent depression is still with us and unemployment in most countries is even worse than in the late 1960s. In 1975, GNP actually fell in all but one of the top ten European OECD countries. I would expect, therefore, that nuptiality will not recover until the economy improves. In Britain this may happen in 1978—NIESR (1977) estimates personal disposable income down ½% in 1976, down 1% in 1977 and up 5% in 1978. Until further radical social as well as economic change occurs in Western Europe, it does not seem likely that the present situation will develop into a marriage pattern on the Swedish model.

There are general structural reasons why high divorce rates may be 'natural' in advanced industrial countries (Künzel, 1974). This follows from the long expectation of life and hence of the life of marriages (doubled since 1891, table 7), small family size and a compressed child bearing period, and the desire of married women

Table 7.   Joint probability of survival of both partners over
30 years of marriage according to period life tables of selected
years, assuming exact age at marriage of husband 25, of wife,
20; England and Wales.

Year	Joint Probability	Year	Joint Probability
1861	0·4914	1945–47	0·7935
1871	0·4523	1950–52	0·8271
1881	0·4957	1955–57	0·8501
1891	0·4832	1961	0·8578
1901	0·5626	1964–66	0·8596
1911	0·6339	1970	0·8641
1921	0·6929	1971	0·8639
1931	0·7153	1972	0·8636
1941	0·7223	1973	0·8644

Source: Calculated from
Registrar-General's Statistical Review Part II appendix B or
Table B1
Keyfitz, N. and W. Flieger (1968) *World Population; an
analysis of vital data*. University of Chicago Press.

to go out to work (Britton, 1976). To this might be added a decline
in religious belief and in traditional morality, exemplified, for
example, in the decline in the frequency of religious ceremonies in
first marriages. Furthermore, low age at marriage will of itself
increase divorce rates. One of the striking facts about the demography of the Western nations is their relative uniformity in most
matters. One might expect that the institutional obstacles which are
partly responsible for current differences in divorce rates will eventually fall to public pressure, and that high levels of divorce will
become general throughout Europe.

Why does marriage matter in demography?

Marriage owes its demographic and genetic importance to its role
as the prime medium of fertility and through the effects of variation in age at marriage on completed fertility. I have discussed the
genetic relationship elsewhere (Coleman, 1977a, b): there is no
space to consider it further here. The relationship has pre-occupied
demographers and was thoroughly investigated by the Royal
Commission on Population (Hajnal, 1950; Glass & Grebenik,
1954). The data collected showed clearly the effect of age at

Table 8a.   Period Total Fertility Rate (legitimate) by age at marriage
of wife; England and Wales.

Age at marriage of wife	TMFR					
	1951	1961	1964	1966	1971	1974
16	4·668	5·114	5·392	5·167	4·427	3·628
20	2·960	3·329	3·440	3·210	2·689	2·190
25	1·701	1·924	1·980	1·808	1·496	1·207
30	0·864	0·905	0·918	0·825	0·626	0·465
35	0·348	0·342	0·340	0·306	0·216	0·142
40	0·084	0·082	0·074	0·067	0·045	0·030
45	0·006	0·005	0·005	0·005	0·003	0·002

Source: Birth Statistics Series FM1 table 3·1 OPCS 1977.

marriage upon fertility by given durations of marriage, especially so upon the incidence of childlessness, particularly in the manual social status groups whose family sizes were larger. It was pointed out that the relationship between fertility and age at marriage, however caused, is likely to be less with smaller average family size. Those marrying early can control their fertility if they wish, those marrying late (as long as it is not too late) will not be prevented by physiological considerations from producing a small family of average size.

However, since the Royal Commission, fertility has increased and Busfield (1972) showed that from 1935 onwards, ratios of fertility at different ages at marriage by 10 years marriage duration have not diminished. This is still true for the most recent data available (see table 8) except for women married in their teens. If there is a general reluctance to extend childbearing much past age 30, and if additionally there is a tendency to compress family building into the first 10 years of marriage, then the potential effects of marriage age will be strong. An estimate of the statistical effect of changes in marriage on fertility was made by Glass (1971). Comparing the distributions of age at first marriage for women married in 1931 and in 1950, and the cumulative fertility rates for the 1931 and 1956 marriage cohorts at successive ages of marriage, he estimated that 30% of the increase in live births per married woman between those cohorts at 10 years marriage duration was accounted for by the fall in the age at marriage. Another way of

Table 8b. Average number of liveborn children per married woman. First marriages, marriage cohorts 1925–1964, marriage duration 10 years; England and Wales.

(1) Actual Data

Year of marriage	Age at marriage						
	<45	<20	20–24	25–29	30–34	35–39	40–44
1925	1·72	2·38	1·93	1·48	1·28	0·79	0·39
1930	1·64	2·38	1·81	1·44	1·10	0·67	0·27
1935	1·60	2·31	1·76	1·42	1·10	0·54	0·27
1940	1·63	2·08	1·73	1·50	1·16	0·61	0·24
1945	1·79	2·22	1·85	1·69	1·33	0·73	0·25
1950	1·84	2·41	1·89	1·50	1·32	0·68	0·22
1955	1·99	2·45	2·00	1·83	1·40	0·74	0·23
1960	2·13	2·50	2·11	1·99	1·57	0·80	*
1964	2·02	2·25	2·01	1·89	1·49	0·81	*

(2) Proportional Data: 20–24 rates as 100

Year of marriage	Age at marriage						
	<45	<20	20–24	25–29	30–34	35–39	40–44
1925	89	123	100	77	66	41	20
1930	91	131	100	80	61	37	15
1935	91	131	100	81	63	31	15
1940	94	120	100	87	67	35	14
1945	97	120	100	91	72	39	14
1950	97	128	100	79	70	36	12
1955	100	123	100	92	70	37	12
1960	101	118	100	94	74	38	*
1964	100	112	100	94	74	40	*

Source: Birth Statistics 1974 Series FM1,1 table 10·4 pp. 91–93
* = not available.
Registrar-General's Statistical Review 1969 Part II table QQ(b) pp. 174–179.

showing the potential effect is to apply age-specific marital fertility rates of given years by the proportion married in each age group, not of the proper years, but of 1921, 1931 and 1951. Without the decline in age at marriage, the number of births per year on these assumptions would be up to 40% less than actually occurred (table 9).

Divorce is usually assumed to have a negative effect upon fertility by exposing women to situations where they would be unlikely or unwilling to conceive. For example, Cohen and Sweet (1974) showed for American women married in 1965 aged 25–54

Table 9. Comparison of legitimate births for selected years with the numbers of births expected from a married population standardized on the proportions married by age in 1921, 1931 and 1951; England and Wales.

		1951	1961	1964	1966	1971	1972	1973	1974
Actual births		644 758	762 791	812 632	782 767	717 477	662 929	617 856	583 399
Births expected from population standardized on 1921, 31 and 51, and as % of actual births	(1) 1921	469 537	484 990	502 252	470 077	415 167	387 423	364 600	349 338
		72·8%	63·6%	61·8%	60·1%	57·9%	58·4%	59·0%	59·9%
	(2) 1931	475 713	488 220	508 408	474 992	420 156	391 585	368 914	353 677
		73·8%	64·0%	62·6%	60·7%	58·6%	59·1%	59·7%	60·6%
	(3) 1951	650 791	674 087	710 179	672 797	602 546	561 169	526 392	505 079
		100·9%	88·4%	87·4%	86·0%	84·0%	84·6%	85·2%	86·6%

Sources: OPCS (1977) Birth Statistics 1974 Series FM1, table 31, p. 20. OPCS (1977) Marriage and Divorce Statistics Series FM2,1 1974 table 3·1 p. 20. Census of England and Wales 1961. Age, Marital Condition and General Tables, Table 12, p. 34, Table 9, p. 30.

that those whose first marriage was terminated by divorce had 0·14 children less than those with uninterrupted first marriages. When corrected for age at marriage, this deficit rose to 0·6 children. But when corrected for the time spent separated before divorce, the deficit falls to only 0·1. Registrar-General's data for England and Wales shows higher childlessness and lower mean fertility of divorced couples (at time of decree absolute) compared to contact marriages of the same average duration (table 10). This is an undoubted effect of divorce upon fertility, but the American data make it less clear that fertility has an important effect upon divorce, once the period of separation is accounted for. Further-more, some European data seem to suggest that fertility differen-tials between the divorced and still-married are declining as time goes on. In West Germany in 1953 divorced couples had 1·03 children compared to 1·24 in intact marriages (83%) while in 1963 the corresponding figures were 1·22 compared to 1·35 (Festy & Prioux, 1975). Even if childless couples were originally conspi-cuously vulnerable to divorce, as divorce becomes more generally

Table 10.   Fertility of Divorced Couples; England and Wales.

Year of divorce	No. of couples divorced	Proportion childless (%)	Mean No. of children			Average duration of marriage at divorce
			All div. couples	Fertile div. couples	All first marriages*	
1964	34 868	30·1	1·44	2·07	2·04	12·9
1965	37 785	29·0	1·48	2·09	2·09	12·9
1966	39 067	28·2	1·53	2·13	2·13	12·8
1967	43 093	27·4	1·57	2·16	2·16	12·8
1968	45 794	26·9	1·59	2·17	2·17	12·7
1969	51 310	27·1	1·58	2·17	2·22	12·5
1970	58 239	26·1	1·61	2·18	2·23	12·3
1971	74 437	27·5	1·57	2·16	2·26	13·6
1972	119 025	25·9	1·64	2·22	2·25	14·3
1973	106 003	24·8	1·70	2·26	2·28	13·3
1974	113 500	25·4	1·68	2·25	2·23	13·0

*Mean number of liveborn children at 13 years marriage duration (first marriages unbroken by divorce).

Source: Birth Statistics 1974 Series FM1,1 table 10.4 p. 91 Marriage and Divorce Statistics 1974 Series FM2,1 table 4·3 p. 42, table 4·5a p. 46.

popular it is to be expected that more couples of normal fertility will become divorced. So at least in those countries where juvenile cohabitation and illegitimate births are relatively infrequent, marriage and marriage-age still seem to be necessary categories in the study of fertility.

Summary

Three phases are evident in marriage patterns in all European countries. First, a continuation into the 1930s of the traditional West European marriage pattern of high age at marriage and relatively low proportions ever-married; secondly, a fall in mean age at marriage and an increase in proportions marrying in successive marriage cohorts for the 1930s onward—the latter being particularly marked for women as the sex ratio has moved in their favour; thirdly, a partial reversal of these trends in the late 1960s and in the 1970s, particularly in Sweden and Denmark, where a new pattern of cohabitation and childbirth outside marriage is becoming popular.

The pattern of divorce differs from that of nuptiality in that its absolute level differs greatly between different countries, as its incidence is much affected by legal provisions. Most countries have shared an upward trend which accelerated rapidly in the late 1960s, both before and especially after radical divorce law reform. At present rates more than one third of marriages in the United Kingdom, in Scandinavian countries and in the USA may be expected to end in divorce.

The postwar rise in the popularity of marriage may be regarded as a final stage in the completion of the demographic transition—the very recent fall in marriage rates probably being a temporary response, at least outside Scandinavia, to unusually unfavourable economic conditions. In England and Wales at least, marriage remains the predominant setting for fertility and the relation between fertility and age at marriage remains strong. Consequently it remains an important category in demographic analysis.

Acknowledgements

I am grateful to the staff of the OPCS for providing me with unpublished data, and to the SSRC for a grant towards the Reading Marriage Survey 1974.

References

AKERS, D. S. (1967) On measuring the marriage squeeze, *Demography*, **4**,2, 907–924.

BARNETT, C. (1972) *The Collapse of British Power*. Methuen, London.

BECKER, G. S. (1973) A Theory of Marriage Part I, II, *Journal of Political Economy*, **81**, 4, 5.

BERKNER, L. K. (1973) Recent research on the history of the family in Western Europe. *Journal of Marriage and the Family*, **35**, 3, 395–405.

BANKS, J. A. (1954) *Prosperity and Parenthood*. Routledge and Kegan Paul, London.

BRAHIMI, M. (1978) Nuptialité et fécondité en Irlande, *Population*, **33**, 663–703.

BRITTON, M. (1976) Women at work. *Population Trends*, **2**, 22–25, HMSO, London.

BUSFIELD, J. (1972) Age at marriage and family size: social causation and social selection hypotheses. *Journal of Biosocial Science* 4, 1, 117–134.

CHESTER, R. (1971) The duration of marriage to divorce. *British Journal of Sociology*, **22**, 172–182.

COHEN, S. B. and SWEET, J. A. (1974) The impact of marital disruption and remarriage on fertility. *Journal of Marriage and the Family*, **36**, 1, 87–96.

COLEMAN, D. A., (1977a) Assortative mating in Britain. In Chester, R. and Peel, J. (eds) *Equalities and Inequalities in Family Life*, Academic Press, London.

COLEMAN, D. A. (1977b) Marriage and mobility in Britain—secular trends in a nationwide sample. *Annals of Human Biology*, **4**, 4, 309–330.

DEANE, P. and COLE, W. A. (1969) *British Economic Growth 1688–1959*. Cambridge University Press.

DEPARTMENT OF HEALTH AND SOCIAL SECURITY (1974) Report of the Committee on One-Parent Families, Vol. 1, CMND 5629, HMSO, London.

FARID, S. M. (1976) Cohort nuptiality in England and Wales. *Population Studies*, **30**, 1, 137–151.

FESTY, P. (1971) Evolution de la nuptialité en Europe occidentale depuis la guerre. *Population*, **26**, 3, 331–379.

FESTY, P. (1973) Canada, United States, Australia and New Zealand Nuptiality Trends. *Population Studies*, **27**, 3, 479–492.

FESTY, P. and PRIOUX, F. (1975) Le Divorce en Europe depuis 1950. *Population Studies*, **30**, 6, 975–1003.

GIBSON, C. (1974) The association between divorce and social class in England and Wales. *British Journal of Sociology*, **25**, 79–93.

GLASS, D.V. (1938) Marriage frequency and economic fluctuations in England and Wales 1854–1937 in Hogben, L. (ed) *Political Arithmetic*. Allen and Unwin.

GLASS, D. V. (1971) The components of natural increase in England and Wales. In *First Report of the Select Committee in Science and Technology. Population of the United Kingdom*. HMSO, London.

GLASS, D. V. (1976) Recent and prospective trends in fertility in developed countries. *Philosophical Transactions of the Royal Society B*, **274**, 1–52.

GLASS, D. V. and GREBENIK, E. (1954) *The Trend and Pattern of Fertility in Great Britain*, Vol. 1, 2. Papers of the Royal Commission on Population, Vol. VI, HMSO, London.

GREBENIK, E. and ROWNTREE, G. (1963) Factors associated with age at marriage in Britain. *Proceedings of the Royal Society B*, **159**, 178–197.

GLICK, P. C. and NORTON, A. J. (1973) Perspectives on the recent upturn in divorce and remarriage. *Demography*, **10**, 3, 301–314.

HAJNAL, J. (1947) Aspects of recent trends of marriage in England and Wales. *Population Studies*, 1, 1, 72–98.
HAJNAL, J. (1950) *Births, Marriages and Reproductivity in England and Wales 1938–1947.* Papers of the Royal Commission on population II. Reports and Selected Papers of the Statistics Committee.
HAJNAL, J. (1953) Age at marriage and proportions marrying. *Population Studies*, 7, 1.
HAJNAL, J. (1965) European marriage patterns in perspective in Glass, D.V. and Eversley, D. E. C. (eds) *Population in History.* Arnold, London.
HENRY, L. (1975) Schema d'évolution des marriages après de grandes variations des naissances, *Population*, 30, 4/5, 759–779.
IMMIGRANT STATISTICS UNIT (1978) Marriage and birth patterns among the New Commonwealth and Pakistani populations. *Population Trends*, 11, 5–9, HMSO, London.
INED (1977) Sixième rapport sur la situation démographique de la France. *Population*, 32, 2, 255–338.
KUNZEL, R. (1974) The connection between the family cycle and divorce rates. An analysis based on European data. *Journal of Marriage and the Family*, 36, 2, 379–388.
LASLETT, P. (1965) *The World we have Lost.* Methuen, London.
LEETE, R. (1976) Marriage and divorce trends and patterns. *Population Trends*, 3, 3–8. HMSO. London.
LEETE, R. (1977a) Changing patterns of Marriage and Re-marriage. In Chester, R. and Peel, J. (eds) *Equalities and Inequalities in Family Life.* Academic Press, London.
LEETE, R. (1977b) Changing marital composition. *Population Trends*, 10, 16–21, HMSO, London.
LEETE, R. (in the press) Changing patterns of family formation and dissolution in England and Wales 1964–1976: evidence from marriage and divorce statistics *OPCS Studies on Medical and Population Subjects no. 39*, HMSO, London.
MAISON, D. (1974) Ruptures d'union par décès ou divorce. *Population*, 29, 2, 249–262.
MAISON, D. and MILLETT, E. (1974) La population de la France. La nuptialité. *Population*, 29, Numero Special, 31–50.
MUHSAM, H. V. (1974) The Marriage Squeeze. *Demography*, 11, 2, 291–299.
NATIONAL INSTITUTE FOR ECONOMIC AND SOCIAL RESEARCH (1977) *Economic Review* 1977, NIESR, London.
OPCS (1977a) Birth Statistics. *Series FM1*, 1, HMSO, London.
OPCS (1977b) Marriage and Divorce Statistics, *Series FM2*, 1, HMSO, London.
OPCS (1977c) Monitor FM2 77/4 Marriages 1975 and 1976. Information Branch OPCS, London.
OPCS (1977d) *Monitor FM2 77/3* Divorce 1975 and 1976.
OPCS (1977e) *Monitor R09 77/3* New Population estimates for England and Wales mid-1971 to mid-1976.
PEARCE, D. and FARID, S. (1977) Illegitimate births—changing patterns, *Population Trends*, 9, 20–23.
PRIOUX-MARCHAL, F. (1974) Le mariage en Suède. *Population*, 29, 4–5, 825–853.
PRIOUX, F. (1977) La situation démographique des pays Nordiques, *Population*, 32, 1, 139–174.
RAYNER, C. (1973) On the 25 + shelf. *New Society*, 13 December 1973.
REGISTRAR-GENERAL (1963) *Registrar-General's Statistical Review for 1961. Part III, Commentary.* HMSO, London.

REGISTRAR-GENERAL (1971) *Registrar-General's Statistical Review of England and Wales 1969. Part II, Population*, HMSO, London.

REGISTRAR-GENERAL (1971) *Registrar-General's Statistical Review of England and Wales 1967. Part III, Commentary*, HMSO, London.

ROUSSEL, L. (1977) Démographie et mode de vie conjugale en Danemark. *Population*, 32, 2, 339–359.

ROUSSEL, L. (1978) La cohabitation juvenile en France. *Population*, 33, 1, 15–42.

ROWNTREE, G. (1962) New facts on teenage marriage. *New Society*, 3, 12–15.

ROWNTREE, G. and CARRIER, N. (1958) The resort to divorce in England and Wales 1858–1957. *Population Studies*, XI, 3, 188–232.

RYDER, N. B. (1963) Measures of recent nuptiality in the Western World. *Proceedings of the International Population Conference*, New York, 1961. Vol. 2, 293–301, IUSSP, London.

SCHOEN, R. and NELSON, V. E. (1974) Marriage, divorce and mortality, a life table analysis. *Demography*, 11, 2, 267–290.

SCHOFIELD, M. (1965) *The Sexual Life of Young People*. Penguin, Harmondsworth.

SHORTER, E., KNODEL, J. and VAN DE WALLE, E. (1971) The decline of non-marital fertility in Europe 1880–1940. *Population Studies*, 25, 375–393.

SHRYOCK, H. S. and SIEGEL, J. S. (1975) *The Materials and Methods of Demography*, Vol. 2. US Department of Commerce Bureau of the Census. US Government Printing Office, Washington DC.

SILVER, M. (1966) Births, marriages and income fluctuations in the United Kingdom and Japan. *Economic Development and Cultural Change*, 14, 302–333.

SPENGLER, J. J. (1972) Demographic factors and early modern economic development in Glass, D. V. and Revelle, R. (eds) *Population and Social Change*, Arnold, London.

STATISTICS OFFICE, DUBLIN *Southern Ireland Report on Vital Statistics 1974.*

TANNER, J. M. (1973) Trend towards earlier menarche in London, Oslo, Copenhagen, the Netherlands and Hungary. *Nature*, 243, 95–9.

THOMAS, D. S. (1927) *Social Aspects of the Business Cycle*. New York, Gordon and Breach, A. A. KNOPF.

TOMASSON, R. F. (1977) A Millenium of misery: the demography of the Icelanders. *Population Studies*, 31, 3, 405–428.

VAN DE WALLE, J. (1972) Marriage and marital fertility. In Glass, D.V. and Revelle, R. (eds) *Population and Social Change*. Arnold, London.

WINTER, J. M. (1976) Some aspects of the demographic consequences of the first world war in Britain. *Population Studies*, 30, 3, 539–551.

SEX DIFFERENTIALS AND CAUSE OF DEATH IN SOME EUROPEAN COUNTRIES

GUILLAUME WUNSCH

Département de Démographie, Université Catholique de Louvain

Introduction

Trends in age–sex mortality in developed countries during the last decades have been well described in various publications †. Most notable has been the gap between male and female mortality, already documented two decades ago by M. Spiegelman (1955) amongst others, which one can trace back in many cases to the fall in mortality, in the late 19th or early 20th century, and which has continued to widen during the last decades. For example, the difference in male and female expectations of life in France has increased from 3·4 years in 1899 to 7·8 years in 1972; the gap between the two mean lengths of life is, however, narrower in some countries such as Sweden.

Another significant factor has been the increase, at certain ages, of the death rates for males; though male infant mortality has continued to decline in developed countries, male death rates have increased recently in various countries in the 15–20, 35–55, and 60–80 age groups. As female death rates have mostly continued to decline, increases in male mortality at these ages have obviously contributed to the widening gap between male and female expectations of life.

As an illustration of the gap between male and female age-specific death rates, we have given in table 1 the arithmetic (unweighted) average and coefficient of variation of the ratio of

---

† Recent contributions include J. Vallin and J. C. Chesnais (1974), and Economic Commission for Europe (1976), chapter III 'Mortality'.

Table 1.   Mean and coefficient of variation of the ratio of male to female death rates, for 25 European countries.

Age groups	1950		1960		1970		1974	
	Mean	C. of V.	Mean	C. of V.	Mean	C. of V.	Mean	C. of V.
0	1·24	0·064	1·25	0·059	1·29	0·073	1·28	0·078
1−4	1·14	0·092	1·21	0·135	1·26	0·147	1·32	0·136
5−14	1·36	0·120	1·54	0·124	1·58	0·112	1·54	0·099
15−24	1·56	0·212	2·24	0·210	2·49	0·170	2·59	0·261
25−34	1·36	0·138	1·71	0·195	2·05	0·205	2·21	0·198
35−44	1·35	0·131	1·47	0·163	1·77	0·196	1·85	0·215
45−54	1·54	0·135	1·65	0·140	1·76	0·146	1·90	0·159
55−64	1·54	0·129	1·78	0·114	1·95	0·117	1·98	0·111
65−74	1·31	0·100	1·48	0·095	1·68	0·099	1·71	0·128
75+	1·11	0·054	1·16	0·055	1·23	0·058	1·25	0·089

of male life-table death rates to female death rates by broad age groups, at specific points in time from 1950 to 1974, for 25 European countries. Data are drawn from the UN Demographic Yearbooks, the WHO Data Bank, and from national sources.

One clearly sees, from table 1, the increase in excess male mortality in all age-groups, the most prominent increases being mainly at young adult ages (15−35) but also in the upper age-brackets excluding the last one, i.e. from 55−75 years of age. The change has been, therefore, typically bimodal, with only virtually nil to small increases at infancy and childhood, in the middle-age group (45−55), and at high ages (above 75).

The geographic dispersion of excess male mortality has, on the other hand, not changed much. There seems to be an increase relative dispersion in some age-groups (35−55, 75+) but no distinct pattern is discernible †.

The rest of this paper will consider in more detail the differences between male and female mortality, and link these differences to differentials by cause of death.

---

† A Wilcoxon matched-pairs signed-ranks test applied to the 1950 and 1970 values shows no significant change, on the whole, at the 0·05 level of significance (two-tailed test).

Changes in sex-differential mortality

Various authors have noted that the gap between male and female .mortality, in developed countries, is independent of the level of mortality. Using data around 1973–74 for 25 European countries, and taking expectation of life at birth as an indication of overall mortality, one observes a very slight correlation (0·12), not statistically significant however, between differences in mean length of life for females and for males, and the level of mortality as measured by the mean length of life for both sexes. The trend in sex-differential mortality may therefore be analysed in a first step without taking into account the level of mortality itself.

Table 2 presents the geometric average of male excess mortality ratios† for 24 European countries.

Table 2 shows that excess male mortality varies widely from one country to another. Around 1974, male excess mortality was especially marked in Finland, Austria, and Norway among others; on the contrary, countries such as Romania, Ireland, Hungary and Yugoslavia have a low level of male excess mortality. Another conclusion which can be drawn from table 2 is that male excess mortality has increased during the period considered in all the countries under observation. Between 1950 and 1970, increases have been especially high in Finland, Austria, Norway and Northern Ireland, but have remained lower in such countries as Scotland, Romania, Belgium, Portugal, and England and Wales. For countries with high excess mortality, the major increase can be ascribed to the 1950–1960 period in Austria and Northern Ireland; in Finland and Norway, similar increases are observed during the 1950s and 1960s. Since 1970, decreases are observed in a few countries, but male excess mortality has increased greatly in Northern Ireland and in Portugal.

---

† Writing $_nt_x$ (M) and $_nt_x$ (F) respectively for the male and female life-table death rates in the age-group x to $x + n$, an average measure of excess mortality by age is given by

$$\left[\prod_{x=0}^{\omega - n} \frac{_nt_x \text{ (M)}}{_nt_x \text{ (F)}} \right]^{1/i}$$

where i stands for the number of age groups considered and ω is the ultimate age of life. See R. Schoen (1970) for the interesting properties of this type of index. For a general discussion of the problem of comparing male and female mortality, see N. Keyfitz and A. Golini (1975), or N. Keyfitz (1977), chapter 3, 54–76.

Table 2.   Geometric average of male excess mortality ratios.

Country	1950	1960	1970	1974
Austria	1·37	1·71	1·82	1·92
Belgium	1·43	1·63	1·69	1·70
Bulgaria	1·27	1·35	1·53	1·59
Czechoslovakia	1·50	1·65	1·80	1·86
Denmark	1·27	1·49	1·55	1·61
Finland	1·54	1·81	2·11	2·02
France	1·42	1·64	1·79	1·86
FR Germany	1·33	1·59	1·70	1·72
Greece	1·27	1·37	1·52	1·60
Hungary	1·31	1·44	1·67	1·53
Ireland	1·15	1·31	1·42	1·51
Italy	1·27	1·48	1·63	1·69
Netherlands	1·29	1·51	1·65	1·69
Norway	1·45	1·68	1·92	1·89
Poland	1·40	1·54	1·75	1·87
Portugal	1·34	1·47	1·58	1·75
Romania	1·25	1·32	1·44	1·45
Spain	1·27	1·41	1·58	1·63
Sweden	1·32	1·47	1·62	1·55
Switzerland	1·40	1·69	1·78	1·78
England & Wales	1·35	1·59	1·60	1·64
N. Ireland	1·23	1·49	1·60	1·83
Scotland	1·43	1·53	1·62	1·61
Yugoslavia	1·19	1·20	1·47	1·54

The indices presented in table 2 are aggregates, covering all age-groups. They conceal major differences in male/female mortality in specific age-groups. Focusing on data arount 1970 in order to retain death rates based on the last round of censuses for most countries, various differentials by age can be noted by observing the excess mortality ratios which, in each age-group, fall outside the interval determined by the mean ± 1 standard deviation. Excluding infant mortality, with its specific problems of endogenous and exogenous mortality †, one notices in the first age group (1 to 5) that all the countries of northern Europe are characterized by male excess mortality indices which are more than one standard deviation from the mean; low male excess mortality is observed, on the other hand, in various Southern and East European countries (Portugal, Romania, Yugoslavia) as well as in Ireland.

† For a good overview of recent trends in infant mortality, see J. Vallin (1976).

Table 3. Countries with high or low male mortality. Percentage of selection.

Low excess mortality		High excess mortality	
Country	%	Country	%
Ireland	20	Finland	21
Romania	17	France	15
Denmark	13	Norway	15
Yugoslavia	13	Austria	9
Bulgaria	10	Czechoslovakia	6
Portugal	10	Poland	6
Greece	7	England & Wales	6
Other[a]	10	Other[b]	22

[a] Sweden, England & Wales, Northern Ireland.
[b] Bulgaria, Denmark, Netherlands, Sweden, Switzerland, Northern Ireland, Scotland.

In the age-groups 5 to 25, high male relative mortality is observed in Austria, Finland and Norway; between 15 and 25, it is also high in Switzerland and Northern Ireland. Male excess mortality is low in Ireland, Portugal, Romania and Yugoslavia, in Sweden between ages 5 and 15, and in Denmark between ages 15 and 25. †

From 25 to 45 years of age, male excess mortality is marked in Czechoslovakia, Poland and, once again, in Finland; it is also observed in Norway between ages 25 and 35. On the contrary, low male relative mortality is observed in both Irelands, as well as in England and Wales, and in Denmark between ages 35 and 45. Between ages 45 and 65, high male relative mortality is observed in Finland; it is also high in France, and in Norway between ages 45 and 55. Ireland and Denmark have slight male excess mortality, as well as Bulgaria, Romania and Yugoslavia in the age-groups 55 to 65. Above age 65, the dispersion of excess mortality ratios is low, France, and England and Wales, have a higher excess male mortality at these ages, while various Southern and East European countries (Bulgaria, Greece, Romania) have a low relative male mortality.

The frequency of selection of the various European countries according to their level of male excess mortality is given in table 3;

† Death rates are low, however, in this age-group so results may tend to be erratic.

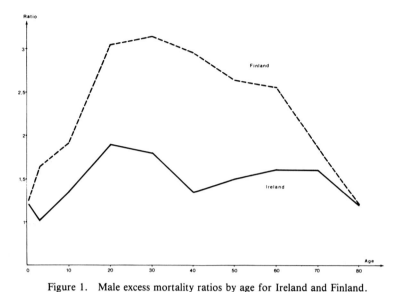

Figure 1.   Male excess mortality ratios by age for Ireland and Finland.

countries not cited in this table fall inside the interval of one standard deviation (plus and minus) from the mean.

It was observed in table 2 that the overall level of male excess mortality, all ages combined, was especially marked in Finland, Norway, Austria and Czechoslovakia. We now see from table 3 that Norway and especially Finland have a high male excess mortality in most age-groups; this is less so for Austria or Czechoslovakia where certain specific age-groups only are concerned. On the other hand, the low male relative mortality countries have a low excess mortality in most age-groups†. As a purely illustrative example of the differential pattern of male excess mortality ratios, figure 1 presents these ratios by broad age-groups, for Finland and Ireland, the two 'leaders' in their respective categories.

The contrast between the two curves is striking; both start and end similarly, but the pattern is completely different: not only are the levels of excess male mortality between 5 and 70 years very different, but the age-schedules of the ratios are discordant.

Obviously, differences between male and female mortality levels

---

† Some countries appear both as having high *and* low excess mortality of males, in table 3. This is due to their differential position according to age, having high ratios at some ages and low ratios at others.

Table 4. Ranks of male and female mean lengths of life and differences between mean lengths (around 1973–74).

Country	Rank of male mean length of life	Rank of female mean length of life	Diference (in years) between female and male mean lengths of life
Austria	15	11	7·3
Belgium	12	12	6·42
Bulgaria	11	15	5·28
Czechoslovakia	20	19	6·96
Denmark	4	5	5·5
Finland	19	10	8·3
France	10	4	7·8
German DR	9	13	5·34
Germany, FR	13	14	6·48
Greece	14	24	3·24
Hungary	17	21	5·72
Ireland	11	20	4·27
Italy	7	9	5·91
Netherlands	3	3	6·0
Norway	2	1	6·28
Poland	18	16	6·93
Portugal	22	22	6·74
Romania	18	23	4·46
Spain	6	8	5·27
Sweden	1	2	5·4
Switzerland	5	6	5·93
England & Wales	8	7	6·2
Northern Ireland	23	17	8·67
Scotland	16	18	6·38
Yugoslavia	21	25	4·8

depend on the two terms of the difference. In other words, a small difference between male and female mortality may be due to a higher than average male mortality or to a lower than average female mortality. It is therefore a useful exercise to try to pinpoint if the difference between both sexes is due primarily to male mortality or on the contrary, to female mortality levels. Taking recent data on expectations of life at birth (around 1973–74), we have ranked the values both for males and females. The agreement between male and female ranking is rather good (the Spearman rank correlation being equal to 0·83), but for various countries the discrepancy between male and female ranks is high. This is particularly the case with Greece, Finland and Ireland, and to a lesser degree with France, Northern Ireland and Romania. According to this procedure,

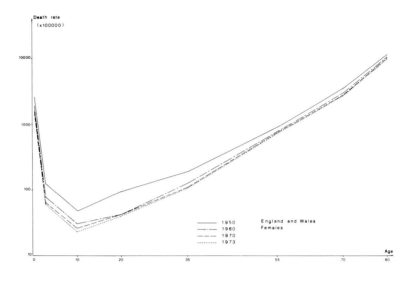

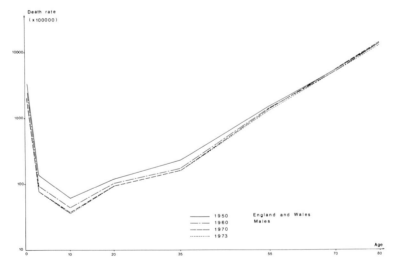

Figure 2.   Death rates by sex and age for England and Wales and for France.

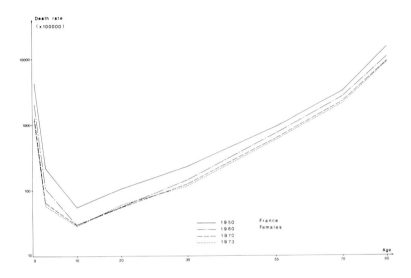

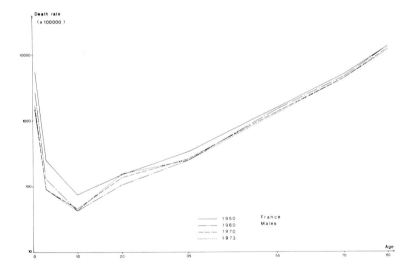

Greece has a low difference between male and female mortality†
due to a high level of female mortality; the same is true of Ireland
and to a lesser degree of Romania. On the other hand, Finland,
Northern Ireland and France have a high male excess mortality
because their expectations of life for males are particularly low
compared to their level of female mortality.

Table 4 presents the ranks of male and female mean lengths of
life around 1973–74, and the corresponding differences between
these mean lengths. High expectations of life correspond in this
table to low ranks, and low expectations to high ranks. Two pairs
of ties appear in the male column, and none in the female column.

Changes in male excess mortality ratios are linked to different
trends in male and female death rates. The age–sex schedules of
period life-table death rates by broad age groups are shown in
figure 2 for two of the most populated countries in Western
Europe, England and Wales, and France. As the scale is loga-
rithmic in ordinate, proportionate changes in rates are reflected by
the graph. As before, four periods were chosen: around 1950, 1960,
1970, and 1974.

From figure 2, one sees that decreases in mortality have usually
been steeper for females than for males; in the cases since 1960
where death rates have actually increased for both sexes, the
increase has usually been more pronounced for males than for
females. Finally, increases in death rates at certain ages during the
last decade have been more frequent for males than for females,
especially as increases in female mortality are restricted to age
groups with low mortality, where results might be somewhat
erratic. These differential changes have therefore led to a deterioration of male excess mortality ratios at all ages.

Before passing on to the next section, where sex-differential
mortality is related to differences in causes of death, we will briefly
place the above results in their historical perspective. If male excess
mortality appears quite generally at all ages in current developed
countries, one must not forget that cases of excess *female* mortality
(at least at certain ages) are not uncommon in developing countries.
Moreover, historical studies for Europe, relating to the 17th and

---

† As measured by the mean lengths of life. Greek mortality data are, however, less
well recorded than for most European countries.

18th centuries clearly point out excess female mortality in reproductive ages and, in some cases, in childhood ages as well. During
the 19th century too, especially after the first quarter of the
century, excess female mortality appears for adolescents and at
reproductive ages, due to differential changes in age-specific death
rates over time, for males and for females. Excess female mortality
at certain ages has disappeared only during the 20th century in
some countries; for example, female excess mortality in the 12 to 16
age-group in France has continued till World War 2 †. The present
situation of male excess mortality at all ages reflects, therefore, an
experience of a half-century only and cannot be considered as a
universal phenomenon.

Sex differential mortality and cause of death

Recent trends in mortality by cause of death in European
countries have been analysed in various publications, for example
in the two papers cited above (Vallin & Chesnais, 1974, and Economic Commission for Europe, 1976), and will not be outlined in
great detail in this contribution. The major findings indicate, over
the past twenty years, an increase in the risks for males of dying
from malignant neoplasms and especially from arteriosclerotic
heart disease. The probability of male survival from accidents and
violence has also deteriorated slightly during the period. On the
contrary, slight improvements have been noted for males, on
average, for other heart and circulatory diseases and for vascular
lesions of the central nervous system.

The situation is, on the whole, better for females: on average,
increases in probabilities of survival are observed for all causes of
death except accidents and violence. For the latter group of causes,
increases in the probability of dying are often more marked for
females than for males. Improvement in female survival is especially noticeable, on average, for vascular lesions of the central
nervous system, and for other heart and circulatory diseases. A
slight increase in survival is also observed for malignant neoplasms
and for arteriosclerotic heart disease.

Changes in the impact of causes of death differ according to age.

---

† For an interesting overview of female excess mortality before the period considered in the present paper, see D. Tabutin (1978).

Table 5.   Geometric average of male to female death rates by cause of death
(around 1970).

Country	Ischaemic heart disease	Cerebro- vascular disease	Other heart and circu- latory dis.	Malignant Neoplasms	Accidents and violence
Austria	3·30	1·35	1·20	1·15	2·60
Belgium	3·21	1·41	1·47	1·14	2·12
Bulgaria	2·14	1·26	1·06	1·28	2·70
Czechoslovakia	3·43	1·48	1·16	1·37	2·56
Denmark	2·46	1·03	1·38	1·27	1·89
Finland	4·94	1·36	1·18	1·37	3·16
France	2·60	1·50	1·46	1·52	2·34
Germany, FR	3·57	1·39	1·22	1·16	2·16
Greece	2·27	1·13	1·27	1·36	2·51
Hungary	2·69	1·23	1·23	1·19	2·40
Ireland	2·77	1·45	1·14	1·08	2·18
Italy	3·30	1·47	0·97	1·32	2·82
Netherlands	4·55	1·00	1·40	1·32	2·04
Norway	4·55	1·50	1·18	1·00	3·16
Poland	3·03	1·34	1·26	1·30	2·88
Portugal	2·24	1·27	1·11	1·05	3·01
Romania	2·12	1·05	1·15	1·21	2·46
Spain	2·84	1·39	1·19	1·28	2·92
Sweden	3·68	0·96	1·79	1·03	2·23
Switzerland	4·02	1·66	1·63	1·14	2·49
England & Wales	2·38	1·11	1·20	1·29	1·90
N. Ireland	3·01	1·14	1·33	1·12	1·73
Scotland	2·34	1·09	1·22	1·55	2·10
Yugoslavia	2·46	1·17	1·08	1·26	2·75

Increases in death rates for males, for example, in the young adult age-groups are essentially due to increases in accidents at these ages. Increases in deaths from arteriosclerotic heart disease, on the other hand, accentuate male mortality mainly above age 45.

We will now compare male and female death rates (3-year averages around 1970) for five major groups of causes of death †. According to the A list of the International Classification of Diseases (8th revision), these are: Ischaemic heart disease (A 83), Cerebrovascular disease (A 85), Other heart and circulatory diseases (A 80–82, 84, 86–88), Malignant neoplasms (A 45–61),

---

† These five groups of causes account for 70 to 75% of all deaths, on average, in European countries. See Economic Commission for Europe, op. cit., p. 40.

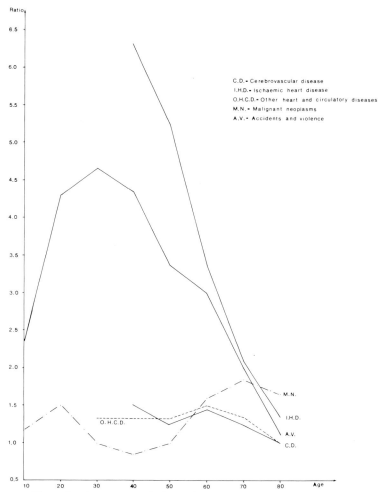

Figure 3. Average age-schedules of male excess mortality ratios (around 1970) for 5 major groups of causes of death and for 24 European countries.

Accidents and violence (AE 138–150). Once again, as in the case of mortality for all causes, ratios of male to female death rates have been summarized by their geometric average. Results are presented in table 5, for 24 European countries.

It is obvious, from table 5, that excess male mortality is

especially high for ischaemic heart disease and for accidents and violence. The impact of the former is, however, greater than that of the latter: not only is the male excess mortality ratio higher for ischaemic heart disease, but the death rate from this disease is much higher than the death rate due to accidents and violence †.

Data in table 5 summarize male excess mortality ratios over all age-groups. Differences appear, however, by age-groups as one can see from figure 3, where the average sex-ratios for 24 European countries (computed around 1970), are presented by age for the five major groups of causes of death given above. As the incidence of the five groups of causes of death varies greatly with age, graphs are restricted to ages with significant death rates due to these causes. One sees, for example, that male excess mortality for ischaemic heart disease decreases with age; the contrary seems to be true for malignant neoplasms. Male excess mortality due to acci-dents and violence is mainly located in the young adult age-groups. No clear pattern by age emerges for cerebrovascular disease and for the other heart and circulatory diseases, except that—at very high ages—the incidents of these diseases seems to be the same for males and for females.

The last characteristic which we will study is the differential impact of the five groups of causes between countries. As before, countries have been classified as having low or high male excess mortality according to their distance from the average age-specific excess mortality ratios computed for the 24 European countries. Once again, analysis will be restricted to the age-groups with signi-ficant levels of death rates.

For malignant neoplasms, Finland has a high male excess mortality in all age-groups above age 25; one can say the same for France between ages 35 and 75. Denmark, Ireland and Sweden, on the other hand, have low excess mortality ratios in most age-groups, especially above age 45.

Male excess mortality for accidents and violence is especially marked, in most age-groups, in Finland, Norway, Poland and Portugal. It is also high in Bulgaria and Yugoslavia at older ages. On the contrary, male excess mortality due to this group of causes

---

† S. Preston (1976) has shown that by far the greatest contribution to sex differential mortality comes from cardiovascular diseases.

is low in most age-groups in Denmark, the Netherlands, and in England and Wales.

Various countries in Northern and Western Europe (Finland especially, and also the Netherlands, Norway, Switzerland) have a high excess male mortality due to ischaemic heart disease, in most age-groups. Several countries in Eastern and Southern Europe (Bulgaria, Hungary, Portugal, Romania, Yugoslavia) have a low male excess mortality due to this cause.

Bulgaria and Romania also have a low male excess mortality due to cerebrovascular disease, contrary to the situation of various West European countries, such as Belgium, France, and the Federal Republic of Germany. Finally, the residual group of all other heart and circulatory diseases shows an excess male mortality above age 45 in Belgium and France especially, and a low male excess mortality in various East and South European countries, as well as in Northern Ireland.

Mortality comparisons by cause of death are usually handicapped by differential diagnostic and coding practices of deaths by cause from one country to another, as well as by changes in the WHO International Classification of Diseases over time. However, as we have focused here on male–female differentials, these sources of bias should not influence our results too much.

Conclusion

In all the developed countries of Europe, male death rates have become greater than female death rates in all age groups. This is due to the fact that, during the last decades, female death rates have decreased more than male death rates; the latter have even increased in certain age groups in most developed countries. Excess male mortality is not a universal phenomenon, however. Female excess mortality can be observed in certain age groups in developing countries; moreover, female excess mortality could also be observed in some age groups in Europe in the 18th and 19th centuries: indeed, in some European countries it has disappeared only before World War 2.

The present situation of male excess mortality can be linked to specific causes of death, particularly to ischaemic heart disease, with its high male excess mortality in the middle age group, to accidents and violence with their peak of excess male mortality at young adult ages, to malignant neoplasms at high ages. These differentials are probably related to types of behaviours which are more frequent in males than in females, such as cigarette smoking, automobile use, alcohol consumption, and working at physically more hazardous jobs (see Waldron, 1976 for an overview). But male–female differential mortality can also be related to more general 'ecological' variables. A recent study has shown, for example, that regional differentials in male and female mortality in Belgium are 'explained' by very different variables (Rapport POLIWA, 1977), male excess mortality being mainly associated with variables of social anomie (i.e. alienation). Behaviours detrimental to health (such as smoking or alcohol consumption) could therefore be considered in many cases as a reaction against social alienation; often they even tend to reinforce integration, as in the case of the social custom of drinking with friends or colleagues. If this is the case, a biomedical approach to male excess mortality is bound to be insufficient; campaigns against smoking or alcohol consumption, for example, may fail in population groups in which these practices constitute a response to social isolation. A new type of approach, incorporating the psycho-social factors determining behaviour, should therefore be envisaged in public health programmes (Waldron & Eyer, 1975; Engel, 1977).

Acknowledgements

The author is grateful to the WHO for providing recent data on deaths by age, sex and cause. He wishes to thank N. Britten and P. M. Boulanger for their helpful suggestions.

References

ECONOMIC COMMISSION FOR EUROPE (1976) 'Mortalité', in Etude sur la situation économique de l'Europe en 1974, 2e partie: *L'évolution démographique de l'Europe depuis la guerre et les perspectives jusqu'en l'an 2000,* Nations Unies, New York, 24–47.

ENGEL, G. L. (1977) The need for a new medical model: a challenge for biomedicine, *Science,* **196**, 4286, 129–136.

Etat démographique de la Wallonie et éléments pour une politique de population. Rapport POLIWA (1977) Département de Démographie, Université Catholique de Louvain, p. 412.

KEYFITZ, N. and GOLINI, A. (1975) Mortality comparisons: the male–female ratio, *Genus,* **XXXI**, 1–4, 1–34.

KEYFITZ, N. (1977) *Applied mathematical demography,* Wiley, New York, p. 388.

PRESTON, S. (1976) *Mortality patterns in national population. With special reference to recorded causes of death.* Academic Press, New York, p, 210.

SCHOEN, R. (1970) The geometric mean of the age-specific death rates as a summary index of mortality, *Demography*, **7**, 3, 317–324.

SPIEGELMAN, M. (1955) An international comparison of mortality rates at the older ages, *Proceedings of the World Population Conference, Rome, 1954*, Vol. 1, United Nations, New York, 289–310.

TABUTIN, D. (1978) La surmortalité féminine en Europe avant 1940, *Population*, **33**, 1, 121–148.

VALLIN, J. and CHESNAIS, J. C. (1974) Evolution récente de la mortalité en Europe, dans les pays anglo-saxons et en Union Soviétique 1960–1970, *Population*, **31**, 4–5, 801–898.

VALLIN, J. (1976) La mortalité infantile dans le monde. Evolution depuis 1950, *Population*, **31**, 4–5, 801–838.

WALDRON, I. and EYER, J. (1975) Socioeconomic causes of the recent rise in death rates for 15–24 yr-olds, *Social Science and Medicine*, **9**, 383–396.

WALDRON, I. (1976) Why do women live longer than men?, *Social Science and Medicine*, **10**, 349–362.

RECENT TRENDS IN MORTALITY AND MORBIDITY IN ENGLAND AND WALES

A. M. ADELSTEIN and J. S. A. ASHLEY

Office of Population Censuses and Surveys, and London School
of Hygiene and Tropical Medicine

Introduction

Analyses of trends in mortality and morbidity (detailed figures and comment) are published regularly by OPCS. In this paper we discuss examples from various recent publications (*The Registrar-General's Decennial Supplement: Occupational Mortality* (1970) OPCS, HMSO; *Area Mortality* (in press) OPCS, HMSO; *Trends in Mortality* (1978) OPCS, HMSO; *Demographic Review* (1978) HMSO.)

Mortality

Death rates

Death rates since 1900 by age, shown in figure 1, are based on Case's generation method—aggregates of 5-year periods in five year age groups both centred on the middle year (Case, 1956); to avoid overcrowding, alternate curves are omitted. Some well-known features are revealed: for young persons there were two exceptions to the regular decline of mortality between successive cohorts, first during the period of World War 1 (with its influenza epidemic), and second a recent rise for young women. The steep decline of mortality after World War 2 is especially clear for young adults, largely from the demise of tuberculosis (Adelstein, 1977). For females this decline eliminated the hump of mortality shown for adolescence and young adulthood in cohorts born during this century. For males the hump, now mainly from violent deaths, remains with a narrower base in younger persons.

145

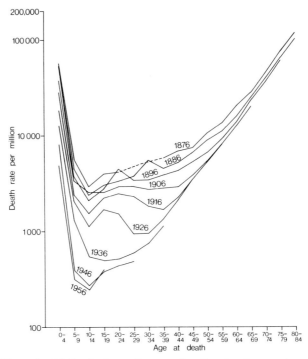

Figure 1.   (a) Deaths from all causes, for all males. 5 year cohorts by
median year of birth.

For older persons the patterns of falling mortality differ between
the sexes. For successive cohorts of females born before 1916, the
fall is consistent and much greater than for men. But the line for
the 1916 female cohort meets its predecessor at age 50, and from this
point the picture begins to resemble that of the men of earlier
cohorts in which successive cohort curves bunch together, each
joining its predecessor at a younger age. Seen as a generation
process, the decline in mortality of women above middle age (other
things staying equal) could be ending, following the established
pattern of men's mortality.

Sex ratio

The ratio of M/F death rates is shown in figure 2. It had been
increasing during the last 50 years especially in two age groups,
round about 20 and 60 years. The first, in young adults, is due

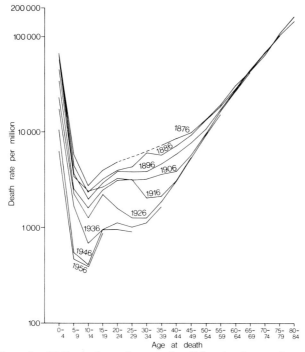

Figure 1.   (b) Deaths from all causes, for all females. 5 year cohorts by median year of birth.

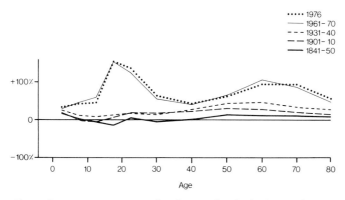

Figure 2.   Percentage excess of male over female death rates by age, 1841–1976.

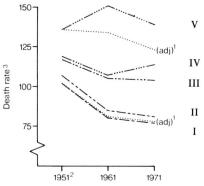

Figure 3.   Recent trends in death rates by social class, 1951–1971, men
aged 15–64.
[1] 1961 and 1971 rates for social classes I and V were adjusted to the 1950
classifications.
[2] 1951 rates were adjusted for errors to company directors and changes to
social class IV.
[3] Direct age-standardized death rate per 100 000 living at ages 15–64
using all men in 1970–72 as the standard.

almost entirely to the difference between sexes in violent deaths; at
age 60 the difference is attributable mainly to coronary heart
disease and lung cancer, and this rise in the all-causes ratio during
this century reinforces the credence we place on the figures showing
the excessive rise of these diseases in men. The M/F ratio around
age 60, which had reached over 2, now seems to be receding
slightly.

Social factors

In the middle of the last century, Farr had shown that health was
related to environment and to life style, and, since 1911, the Registrar-General has periodically published mortality analyses by socio-
economic groupings based on occupations. From the· very first
these analyses have always shown a social class gradient (high in V)
in overall mortality, although for some particular causes of death
the gradient was reversed. The gradient upward from I to V, is
present throughout the lifespan in either sex. In 1971 the spread is
greatest at age 20–34 (*Occupational Mortality*, 1978).

Comparisons of the variation between classes over time are
bedevilled by changes in classifications and changes in the distribution

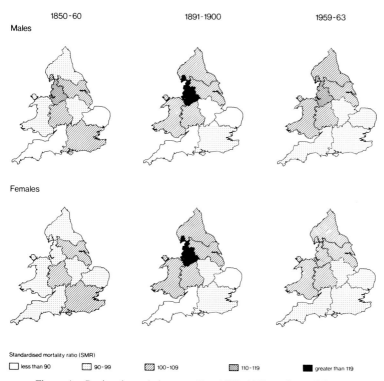

Figure 4.   Regional trends in mortality, 1850–1963, males and females
at all ages.

of persons by occupations. For example, the proportion of all men
aged 16–64 who were in social class V has fallen from some 16% in
1931 to about 7% in 1971. Figure 3 shows age standardized death
rates around 1951, 1961 and 1971 for men aged 15–64, by social
class. In addition to the observed values the figure includes values
which have been adjusted to conform as far as possible to previous
classifications. The apparent rise in mortality of men in social class
IV in 1971 can be attributed to the inclusion of men who formerly
would have been in class V, which is now much smaller and
narrower than it used to be.

   In the 1971 study there are hardly any main categories of disease
with a 'reversed' gradient. The disappearance of the few reversed
gradients could be the result of the more rapid spread of adverse

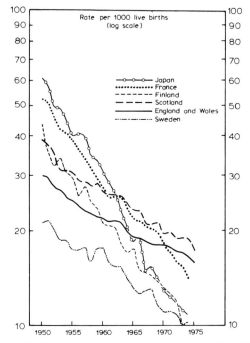

Figure 5.   Infant mortality in selected countries, 1950–1975.

effects of affluence to classes previously spared—manual workers.

Given a relationship between health and achievement, part of this persistence of the differences in mortality between classes is self-fulfilling—healthier persons on average climb the social ladder (say between censuses) and sick persons stay or drift down: this selection process is probably most effective against the relatively small numbers now in class V.

Geographic differences

Figure 4 shows that the differences of mortality rates between regions, broadly speaking, have been relatively steady over the century. The relative position of London has improved but Wales and the North Region have deteriorated, and Lancashire in the North-West has remained poor. The rising gradient of mortality from South to North continues in Scotland. Within regions,

Table 1. Age-specific mortality ratios, 1911, 1931, 1970.

Males		0−4	5−24	25−44	45−64	65−74	75+
Conurbations	1911	109	105	106	112	110	104
	1931	109	102	104	109	109	105
	1970	110	97	106	106	107	104
Rural districts	1911	73	85	81	73	82	95
	1931	80	89	83	80	85	95
	1970	85	110	90	88	88	94

Females		0−4	5−24	25−44	45−64	65−74	75+
Conurbations	1911	110	101	109	106	103	
	1931	109	102	100	104	108	103
	1970	110	100	108	103	101	100
Rural districts	1911	69	90	92	80	86	94
	1931	81	93	97	91	89	97
	1970	87	99	90	93	95	101

variations in rates between social classes are relatively constant; the two factors, region and class, are largely independent, and the geographic gradient in male mortality of adults owes hardly anything to social class distributions. However, the geographic distribution of infant mortality is partly related to social class of fathers. The cause of the geographic variations in mortality is not clear; migration, standards of living, relative urbanization, climate, and quality of water, have been suggested; migration of the healthy seems to be the current favourite.

Urban−rural differences

Table 1 shows the mortality ratio in ages by aggregations of populations in 1921 and 1971. While SMRs are generally highest in conurbations and lowest in rural areas, this is not so in all age groups. For males at ages 5−24, the mortality rates of rural areas are high because of more accidents; this is so for every region, East Anglia and Wales having the highest overall death rates at this age.

International comparisons

Table 2 shows, for 1901 and 1974 within each age-group, how the death rates of England and Wales rank among 11 countries. On the whole, England and Wales has improved its position over the

Table 2.   Mortality rates of England and Wales ranked among nine countries (Scotland, Ireland, Denmark, Sweden, Italy, France, Australia, New Zealand).

Age	0	1-4	5-14	15-24	25-34	35-44	45-54	55-64	65-74	75	Total
1900 Males	N/A	N/A	5	3	4	7	8	8	8	5	6
-02 Females	N/A	N/A	3	2	2	5	7	7	6	6	4
1974 Males	6	4	2	1	1	1	4	7	7	6	8
Females	6	3	5	2	2	4	5	5	6	5	8

period, but the table does not show recent trends in infant mortality for which we have fallen behind (see Figure 4). Mortality in England and Wales is especially favourable between ages 5 and 44, but this advantage is lost after middle age.

General

Why have death rates for men of middle age and above in England and Wales not declined more in recent times? On the one hand, better standards of life have brought taller, healthier young people, more resistant to infections, and antibiotics have helped to control many infections which were formerly the major causes of death. But, on the other hand, older persons had already been damaged by earlier infections as well as by chronic diseases brought about by cumulative processes, most of which were not alleviated by the 'improved' health of young persons; some remained (e.g. effects of early malnutrition) and some cumulative processes appear to have been increasing, e.g. cardiovascular disease, diabetes, and lung cancer. Also, some of the young persons saved by therapy might be left with shorter remaining life spans than average; as an example, Armstrong et al. showed relatively high death rates of a group of diabetics whose records were assembled in 1964 (Armstrong, Lea, Adelstein, Donovan, White, & Ruttle, 1976).

It would seem to be clear that, during this century, potential improvements in health have been offset in later life by chronic progressive disorders and the spread to all social classes of the so called affluent diseases. After middle age the main causes of death changed, and the net gain was small.

One of the achievements of epidemiology has been to show that many of these chronic disorders, including some cancers are not simply due to ageing; they are caused by environmental hazards or particular diets, smoking practices, or other aspects of life style such as patterns of breeding, or by the rat-race inducing what is loosely called stress.

There is hardly a chronic disease, however rampant in some places, that is not insignificant in others, sometimes even in the same country; disease rates vary between social groupings; many disease patterns of immigrants gradually converge with those of their hosts; incidence may be correlated with environmental changes. It augurs well for the future that much is now known about the relationships of diseases with life style. Even so, the improvement may be slow because many harmful activities like smoking and drinking too much seem to be irrational and are the products of other, deeply rooted, social customs which are not easily changed.

Since heart disease and cancer (especially of bronchus and lung), which are important causes of continuing high death rates above middle age, seem to be mostly preventable, we shall now discuss them in more detail.

Heart and blood vessels

A feature of the changed causes of mortality after middle age, particularly in men, is the increase attributed to diseases of the heart and blood vessels, mainly disease of the coronary arteries, e.g. coronary thrombosis or ischaemic heart disease.

Despite difficulties of interpreting changing trends in diagnoses, it seems clear that most of this increase is real, as is the decrease in rheumatic heart disease and more recently in hypertensive heart disease.

For women, mortality from cardiovascular disease has always been much lower than for men, but it has been rising. During this century there has been an increasing M/F ratio of death rates from all causes combined; it reaches a peak of about 2:1 at age 60–64 (see figure 2). Virtually all of this increase in the difference in mortality between the sexes can be accounted for by the difference of the rate of rise of mortality from ischaemic heart disease and cancer of the lung and bronchus. A broadly similar picture is present in other countries with advanced economies.

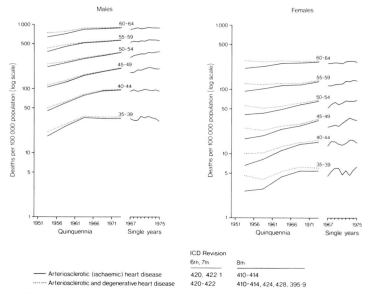

Figure 6.   Ischaemic heart disease. Deaths by age and sex, 1951−75.

In recent years the trend for men has stopped increasing and levelled in most age groups. Only at ages 50−54 is it still rising (figure 6). But in the USA the rising trend has been reversed since about 1963. American authors attribute the decline in male mortality, of some 25% between 1963 and 1975, to changes in diet and smoking (Walker, 1977). If this is correct, we in other countries might hope for a similar change.

Mortality from ischaemic heart disease after World War 2 continued to rise for men, whereas for women it first decreased for some years in all age groups, but since about 1950 has risen for the ages between 35 and 60.

This disorder, responsible for some 30% of deaths of men, is bound up with life style, mainly diet and smoking and, in women, with oral contraceptives. Elsewhere in the world there are communities with exceedingly low incidence. Also, there is evidence that changing life styles by, for example, migration may change its incidence. The diet hypothesis, however, is complex; its newest component, lots of cereal fibre, is, at least, pleasant to take (Morris, Marr & Clayton, 1977).

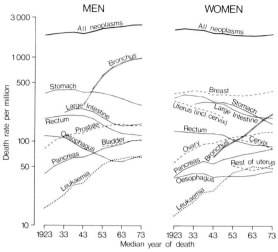

Figure 7. Cancer: standardized death rates, 5 year periods.

Cancers

Although there are considerable differences between them, cancers have enough in common to be classified by the organ in which they arise. Broadly, about 3 out of 10 persons will have contracted cancer in their lives, and two of them will die of it.

In figure 7 mortality rates of cancer have been age standardized, directly, so that they are comparable over time and also between sexes. The overall rate conceals various trends: for men, an enormous rise of cancer of the bronchus and lung: for women the rise came later, and, as yet, is lower. Cancer of the breast, the main cancer for women, is increasing. Other cancers with rising mortality are those of large intestine, pancreas, oesophagus, ovary and testis (not shown in the graph). Mortality (and incidence) of stomach cancer continues to fall sharply, as does cancer of the mouth (not shown) and, less steeply, of the rectum.

Cancer of lung and bronchus

This disease has attracted a great deal of attention, worldwide. It is especially frequent in the UK. As is well known, its frequency is related to environmental factors, by far the most important of which is cigarette smoking. It exemplifies chronic disease directly

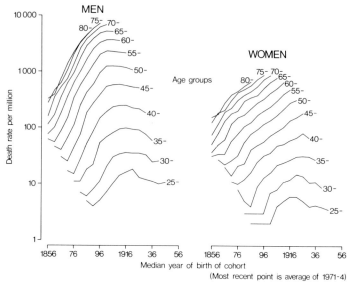

Figure 8.   (a) Death rates for cancer of the lung and pleura.

related to a personal indulgence, solidly embedded in our culture.

Figure 8(a) shows mortality rates in age contours with date of birth on the abscissa. In general the picture, for either sex, is that of a cohort effect. Within each cohort, rates rise with age. For men, rates at each age rise in successive cohorts until those born about 1900 are reached, after which they level out. In later cohorts, there is a moderage decline, so far only affecting men under 65; above this age for men of earlier cohorts it still continues rising. However, the graph does not show a pure cohort effect; there is, in addition, a suggestion of a superimposed time effect seen in that the peaks of successive age contours (beginning at the youngest, 25–29) move to the left.

In figure 8(b) using the same pattern of age contours, are shown figures for cigarette consumption (corrected for tar delivered). Each value is the total cumulated over the lives of the persons up to the stated age (Todd, 1975). For men, the rising trend in smoking in successive generations levels out only after the generation born about 1910. Later some downturn takes place; here, as for men's mortality there is a superimposed time effect.

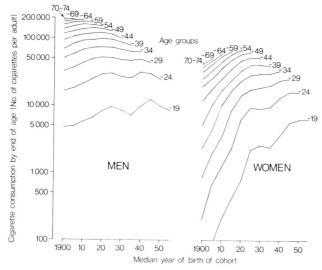

Figure 8. (b) Cumulative cigarette consumption on constant tar basis by cohorts born 1900–55.

Comparing patterns of smoking and mortality, for men, it would appear that there is a factor in addition to smoking, comparatively small, which has introduced the recent downturn of mortality in the younger cohorts.

The mortality of women is lower and the rise in the curves is later and sharper; in every age group death rates rise in successive cohorts, up to the cohort born before about 1920. For cohorts born after about 1920, the curves flatten and then turn down; so far the declining rates have affected women only below 45. The rising trend is consistent with the effects of the rising trend of smoking, but the turndown is not. Here, even more clearly than for men, there would appear to be another factor besides smoking. In a report of the Tobacco Research Council, Todd states that 'in terms of constant tar cigarettes, the continuous increase in cigarette consumption per adult came to an end in 1966'. If these figures published by Todd are taken at face value, there would be a factor besides cigarettes acting before the reduction of smoking; rates of lung cancer are higher in urban areas, and the factor may well be air pollution; reduced pollution could have first checked the previous level of the rise of lung cancer and then reduced it. It must be emphasized, however, that cigarettes are by far the major cause; recent reductions in mortality are relatively small.

Morbidity

It is often suggested that mortality rates in some way indicate community morbidity—the inverse of health. Thus the report of The Resource Allocation Working Party (Department of Health and Social Security, 1976) uses SMRs as weights (among others) for allocating resources between places; and international bodies such as EEC use mortality rates as health indicators. This view has been questioned, and it is difficult, if not impossible, to measure how sensitive mortality is as an indicator of morbidity, precisely because morbidity is itself an elusive concept. Furthermore, much of the available information about morbidity has inherent problems of interpretation.

The most important source of such morbidity information is derived from records of admission to general or psychiatric hospitals, and is usually of high diagnostic quality. In England and Wales the former also has the longest continuous history of morbidity information except that on the incidence of infectious diseases. However, one important aspect of the data, that it relates to individual admissions to hospital rather than to persons, limits its value in the case of chronic disease where the pattern is frequently of multiple admissions. It is also the case that the availability and balance of hospital and other resources can significantly affect the extent to which patients with the same condition are hospitalized; when or where hospital beds are readily available, cases of lesser severity may be admitted whereas if there is a limited supply of beds, admission may be gained only by the more severe cases.

Nevertheless, there is frequently confirmatory evidence of specific rates or trends either from mortality statistics or in comparisons (Royal College of General Practitioners, 1976) derived from the two published National surveys of General Practice carried out in 1955/6 (Logan & Cushion, 1958), and 1970/1 (Office of Population, Censuses and Surveys, 1974). In some cases data from other sources such as the notification of infectious diseases, the registration of malignant diseases, or indeed statistics of sickness absence can also be helpful. However, in this paper we shall particularly refer to the trends as expressed by recent changes

Table 3. Principal decreases in numbers of discharges between 1964 and 1974.

Diagnostic group	Per cent change 1964–74
Other (spontaneous) abortion	— 21
Varicose veins	— 31
Uterovaginal prolapse	— 35
Hypertrophy of tonsils and adenoids	— 47
All tuberculosis	— 51

in the pattern of admission† to hospitals as reported to the *Hospital In-Patient Enquiry* and the *Mental Health Enquiry*.

Falling trends

Some of the alternative explanations for apparently similar trends in General Hospital admissions can be illustrated by considering those few conditions which have shown a fall in the number of admissions to hospitals of this kind during the last decade (table 3): in each case the fall is probably attributable to a different process.

The falling conception rate during the past decade has undoubtably played an important part in the decrease in the number of spontaneous abortions, in that the relationship between the number of abortions reported and the number of births has remained relatively constant during this period (figure 9). Reduction in the birth rate may also have had a small effect in reducing the incidence of varicose veins in women, but this is very unlikely to have significantly affected the number of admissions to hospital. In all probability, most of the recent fall has been due to a change of emphasis in treatment from surgery to sclerosant injection therapy which can be carried out on an out-patient basis or, at most, requires less than a day in hospital. Thus, there has been a greater fall in the rates for women aged between 15 and 44 than for those aged between 45 and 64, (Figure 10) as this form of treatment is, in general, more suitable for younger patients. Nevertheless, the results of the two

---

† Strictly the *Hospital In-Patient Enquiry* relates to *discharges* rather than *admissions* but the two are sufficiently similar that they may be equated.

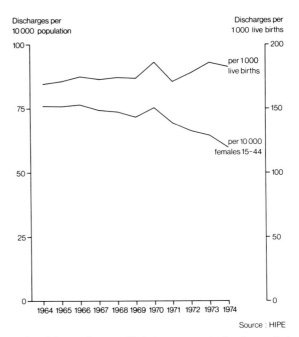

Source : HIPE

Figure 9.   Other and unspecified (spontaneous) abortions: discharge rates, England and Wales, 1964–74.

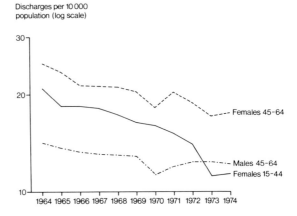

Source : HIPE

Figure 10.   Varicose veins of lower extremities: discharge rates, England and Wales, 1964–74.

Discharges per 10 000
population (log scale)

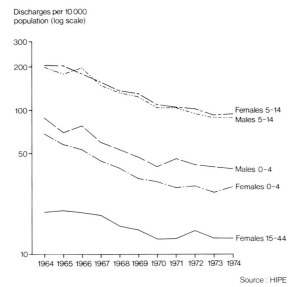

Figure 11.   Hypertrophy of tonsils and/or adenoids: discharge rates,
England and Wales, 1964–74.

National Morbidity studies indicate a 25% fall in the rate of patients consulting at least once with this condition between 1955/6 and 1970/1.

There has also been a profound rise in the extent of day surgery of a variety of kinds during the past few years. In particular, the excisions of benign neoplasms and the performance of a wide range of endoscopic investigations is increasingly being carried out in this way. In consequence, the extent of such work is being monitored in the same way as for in-patients in order that such compensatory changes can be measured.

The drop, in all the relevant age groups, in admissions assigned to hypertrophy of the tonsils and adenoids (figure 11) does not reflect an alteration to another form of therapy of venue of treatment, but more a change of policy as to the effectiveness of the operation of tonsillectomy. Increasingly the need for such operations is questioned and one can foresee the incidence of their performance continuing to fall. Interestingly, the rate of General Practitioner consultations ascribed to this condition also fell profoundly between 1955/6 and 1970/1.

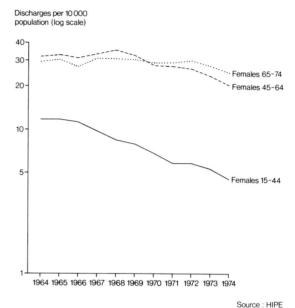

Figure 12.   Uterovaginal prolapse: discharge rates, England and Wales, 1964–74.

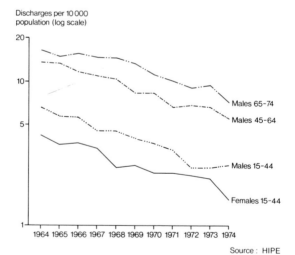

Figure 13.   Tuberculosis of the respiratory system: discharge rates, England and Wales, 1964–74.

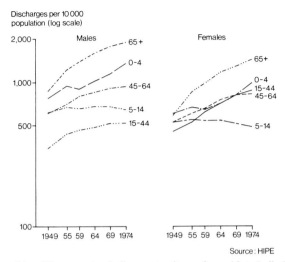

Source: HIPE

Figure 14. All causes (excluding maternity and psychiatry) discharge
rates, England and Wales, 1949–74.

Thus, out of five conditions, only two have shown a fall in the
number of admissions because of a change of incidence. Uterovaginal prolapse has diminished, particularly in younger women
(figure 12), in the main because of a general reduction in fertility
and also perhaps because of increased obstetrical care; and tuberculosis (figure 13) because of the advance of nutrition and of
curative and preventative measures. Both the falls for prolapse and
tuberculosis can be substantiated from other statistical sources.
The reports of the National Morbidity studies show that the rate of
consultation for uterovaginal prolapse halved over the fifteen
years; and the fall in admissions for tuberculosis has been accompanied by parallel falls both in mortality and in notifications of the
disease. This confirms a diminishing incidence rather than, say, the
effect of a greater emphasis on out-patient drug therapy. It should
perhaps be added that there is some evidence of a local resurgence
of the disease in certain sections of the population, but this does
not materially alter the general picture.

Over the past decade, death rates in England and Wales have
fallen or been stationary in every age group, except between the
ages of 20 and 25 where there has been a marginal increase. Yet
between 1964 and 1974 the total number of non-maternity

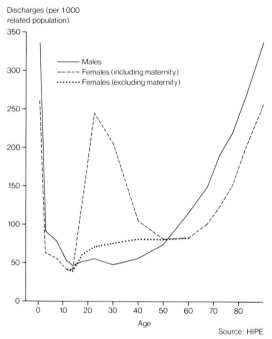

Figure 15.   Hospital discharge rates England and Wales, 1974.

admissions to General Hospitals rose by well over half a million
(19%). However it can be seen (figure 14) that this is a continuation
of a trend stretching over at least the past 25 years during which
much of the increase has occurred in admissions by the very young
and the elderly of both sexes. As a result over the years the U-
shaped curve of admission rates by age (figure 15) has become even
more marked.

Rising trends

It is not surprising to find that those conditions which have
shown the greatest rises over the last ten years (table 4) are
predominantly associated with these age groups. However, other
categories of patients who cannot be classified under a single
diagnostic label have also made significant contributions. In particular the increase in special provision for the newborn, together
with a greater awareness of their needs, has largely been responsible

Table 4.   Principal increases in numbers of discharges between
1964 and 1974.

Diagnostic group	Per cent change 1964–74
Therapeutic abortion	+ 1624
Adverse effects of chemical substances (poisoning)	+ 122
Undescended testicle	+ 86
Fracture of neck of femur	+ 80
Abdominal pain	+ 73
Congenital dislocation of hip	+ 70
Osteo-arthritis and allied conditions	+ 68
Diseases of the ear and mastoid process	+ 66
Acute myocardial infarction	+ 55
Leukaemia	+ 37
Internal derangement of joint	+ 35
Other female genital disorders (gynaecology)	+ 32
All malignant neoplasms	+ 30
Diabetes mellitus	+ 29
Cerebrovascular disease	+ 29

for a marked increase in those 'admitted' to hospital (a subtle difference from being in a nursery attached to a maternity ward) in the first year of life. For example, such admissions doubled between 1964 and 1976.

It is also clear from table 4 that many of the conditions which are highly placed on the list have a generally low mortality and many merit special comment. The most dramatic rise is essentially an artefact in that in 1964, being before the Abortion Act, there were of course negligible numbers of therapeutic abortions.

The highest rates for poisoning occur in the under fives (figure 16) and undoubtably include an undefined, but substantial number of cases of suspected poisoning which are admitted as a precaution. However, the most marked increase in recent years, confirmed in mortality statistics, has been amongst adolescents and young adults, particularly young women. This leads to the suggestion (Alderson, 1974) that this amounts to a cohort effect.

The persistently rising admission rates for undescended testicle and congenital dislocation of the hip are somewhat unexpected, particularly the former during a period when routine school medical examination is declining. One can only speculate that the

166 DEMOGRAPHIC PATTERNS IN DEVELOPED SOCIETIES

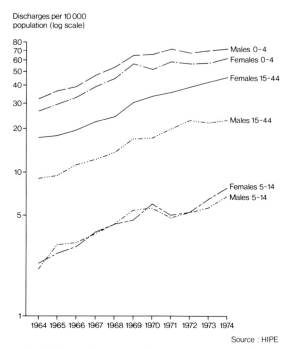

Figure 16. Effects of poisons: discharge rates, England and Wales, 1964–74.

tendency to operate on children for undescended testicle at younger ages is soaking up a 'backlog' which will eventually level out; the rise in dislocation of the hip is thought to be the result of seeking cases rather than a real increase. The rise in the number of cases attributed to diseases of the ear has occurred largely in children and involves removal of adenoids for deafness. It may well be that this is the emergence in the statistics of the condition known as 'glue ear' for which the precise aetiology is still in doubt; alternatively, it could represent a certain amount of reclassification of cases previously specified as hypertrophy of tonsils and adenoids.

In a similar manner, much of the increase in admissions for abdominal pain which occur in childhood is accompanied by an equivalent fall in those attributed to appendicitis (Donnan & Lambert, 1976). This may reflect a diminishing tendency to remove what is subsequently found to be a normal appendix. In addition,

Discharges per 10 000
population (log scale)

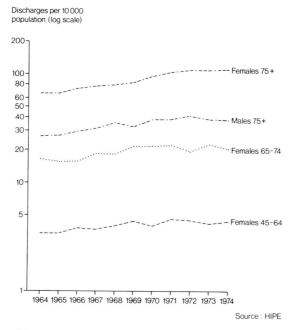

Source : HIPE

Figure 17.   Fracture of the neck of the femur: discharge rates, England and Wales, 1964–74.

however, a substantial number of older cases assigned to this diagnosis are treated in departments of gynaecology, and perhaps are only an alternative manifestation to disorders of menstruation which form the major part of 'other female genital disorders'. The increase in these which has also been noticed by General Practitioners may indicate a lesser tolerance on the part of young women to accept unnecessary discomfort or inconvenience than did the previous generation.

Recent statistics from Mortality and Cancer Registration (Adelstein & White, 1976) do not suggest any rise in the incidence of leukaemia which would account for a rise in admissions. Most of this is attributable to the change of treatment policy, which has of late substituted frequent short admissions for fewer longer ones. In addition, there is probably an increased component of multiple admissions in the case of many malignant neoplasms, although some cancers to which reference has already been made have of

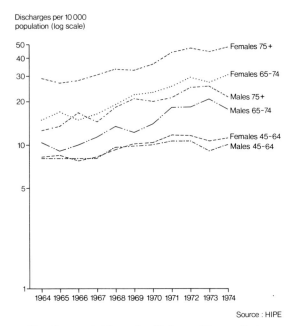

Source : HIPE

Figure 18. Osteo-arthritis and allied conditions: discharge rates,
England and Wales, 1964–74.

course increased over the period, and these are reflected both in
admission and mortality rates. Similarly, recent changes in hospital
admissions, and indeed in General Practice consultations for acute
myocardial infarction, only mirrors the pattern of mortality which
has been previously described.

Much of the recent rise in admissions for fractured femur have
been in very elderly women (figure 17), and the changing age structure within this age group would seem to ensure that the rise will
continue. The elderly have also shown most of the recent increase
in cerebrovascular disease, but it is to be hoped that increasing
control of hypertension will at least tend to slow down this rise, and
perhaps even arrest it. It might be imagined that the past trends in
osteoarthritis would also be similar, but these have clearly been
affected by the development of hip replacement techniques (figure
18). Indeed, the numbers of such operations more than tripled
between 1967 and 1973. It may thus be the awakening of public
awareness of this form of treatment that created a small rise in

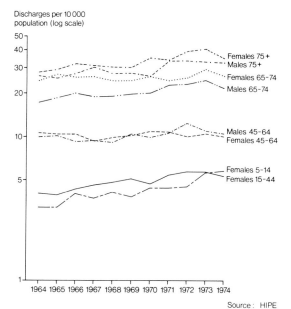

Figure 19. Diabetes mellitus: discharge rates, England and Wales, 1964–74.

General Practitioner consultation rates for this condition in 1970/1. If such techniques continue to gain ground one can foresee that admissions for osteoarthritis and other related conditions may well escalate in the future.

General Practitioners have also recorded increases both in internal derangement of the knee and diabetes. In the case of the former condition one can only speculate about such factors as an increase in sporting or other similar leisure activities. In the case of the latter the incidence is almost certainly rising, particularly in middle age when admission rates are increasing (figure 19). It is, however, surprising that there has been such an increase in admission rates even in these age groups in view of the fact that the general clinical tendency is to aim to prevent admission, apart from those cases who need treatment for diabetic conditions.

Mental illness

One aspect of morbidity for which mortality statistics are particularly inappropriate indicators is that of mental disorders.

General Practitioners reported that consultation rates for these conditions more than doubled between 1955/6 and 1970/1, during a period when the number of admissions to mental illness hospitals and units escalated both in Britain (Department of Health and Social Security, 1977) and the United States (Kramer, 1969). Nevertheless, in more recent years the statistics of admissions show a levelling off of the rates at most ages and a definite fall in rates of first admission to hospital. Within this general pattern, however, it would appear that first admissions by adolescents and young adults are less inclined to fall than those by older adults.

Acknowledgements

We wish to thank our colleagues for help and the Registrar-General for permission to publish.

References

ADELSTEIN, A. M. (1977) Mortality from Tuberculosis. *Population Trends*, **8**, Office of Population Censuses and Surveys. HMSO, London.
ADELSTEIN, A. M. and WHITE, G. C. (1976) Leukaemia 1911–73: cohort analysis. *Population Trends, 3*, 9–13, Office of Population Censuses and Surveys. HMSO, London.
ALDERSON, M. R. C. (1974) Self-poisoning—What is the future? *Lancet*, i, 1040–1043.
ARMSTRONG, B., LEA, A. J., ADELSTEIN, A. M., DONOVAN, J. W., WHITE, G. C. and RUTTLE, S. (1976) Cancer Mortality and saccharin consumption in Diabetes. *British Journal of Preventive and Social Medicine*, **30**.
CASE, R. A. M. (1956) British Journal of Preventive and Social Medicine, **10**.
DEPARTMENT OF HEALTH AND SOCIAL SECURITY (1976) *Sharing resources for health in England*. HMSO, London.
DEPARTMENT OF HEALTH AND SOCIAL SECURITY (various years) *Inpatient statistics from the mental health enquiry for England*. HMSO, London.
DEPARTMENT OF HEALTH AND SOCIAL SECURITY; Office of Population Censuses and Surveys; Welsh Office (various years) *Report of the Hospital Inpatient Enquiry*. HMSO, London.
DONNAN, S. P. B. and LAMBERT, P. M. (1976) Appendicitis: incidence and mortality. *Population Trends, 5*, 26–28. HMSO, London.
KRAMER, M. (1969) Statistics of mental disorders in the United States: current status, some urgent needs and solutions. *Journal of the Royal Statistical Society, Series A*, **132**, 353–407.
LOGAN, W. P. D. and CUSHION, A. A. (1958) *Morbidity Statistics from General Practice*. Studies on Medical and Population subjects No. 14, HMSO, London.
MORRIS, J. N., MARR, J. W. and CLAYTON, D. G. (1977) Diet and Heart. *British Medical Journal, 2*, 1301–1368.
OFFICE OF POPULATION CENSUSES AND SURVEYS (1974) *Morbidity Statistics from General Practice: second national study 1970–71*, Studies on Medical and Population Subjects No. 26. HMSO, London

UK MORBIDITY AND MORTALITY 171

lOFFICE OF POPULATION CENSUSES AND SURVEYS (1978) *Trends in Mortality.* HMSO, London.

The *Registrar-General's Decennial Supplement:* Area mortality, 1969–73 (1979, in the press) Office of Population Censuses and Surveys. HMSO, London.

The *Registrar-General's Decennial Supplement:* Occupational Mortality, 1970–72 (1978) Office of Population Censuses and Surveys. HMSO, London.

The *Registrar-General's Demographic Review* (1978, in the press) Office of Popula-tion Censuses and Surveys. HMSO, London.

TODD, G. F. (1975) Changes in smoking patterns in the United Kingdom. *Tobacco Research Council,* Occasional Paper 1. London.

WALKER, W. J. (1977) Changing United State's Life-style and declining vascular mortality. *New England Journal of Medicine.*

THE FEAR OF POPULATION DECLINE
IN WESTERN EUROPE, 1870-1940

J. M. WINTER

Department of Social History, University of Warwick, Coventry
(Present address: Department of History, University of Cambridge)

Three elements combined in the two generations between 1870 and 1939 to provide a firm basis for the widespread expression of fears of population decline in Western Europe. The first was the fact of waning rates of natural increase in France and Britain from the 1870s, which was noticed with alarm by doctors, scientists, churchmen, politicians, and other interested parties. The second was the development and wide dissemination in the late nineteenth and early twentieth century of genetic theories which seemed to permit analysis of the hereditary character of social behaviour. These ideas helped transform discussions of population growth into arguments about the perceived decline of the inherent qualities of élites, nations, or races. The third was the appearance and growth of an international labour movement, whose potential power was distinctly unsettling to large sections of the educated middle class and its political spokesmen.

The fusion of these three components of the fear of population decline took place in many guises and with many variations. Agreement on this one question did not preclude fundamental opposition on virtually every other social and political issue. But by the mid-1930s, and in particular by the end of World War 2, the ground was cut from under each of these pillars of pessimism. Firstly, the recovery of fertility rates in the late-1930s and. in the postwar years, which may have been a temporary phenomenon, led some writers to consider the period 1870–1939 as a discrete phase of demographic history which, they noted with relief, had apparently come to an end. Secondly, research in genetics in the period 1900–40 threw considerable doubt on the adequacy of early theories of the hereditary character of disease, deviance, or social success, however defined.

These two changes affected a relatively small proportion of the population concerned with declining rates of natural increase. The third had a much wider effect. For after the rise of Hitler, it was not possible for conservatives to advocate openly the sterilization of prolific social misfits, or to voice publicly their alarm at the dangerous fertility of the working class and the suicidal infertility of their social superiors. A change in the language of political discourse had important implications for general discussions of population problems. If the Nazis can be said to have achieved anything beneficial, it was to discredit politically and socially an attitude which expresses social fear in biological or racial language. Prewar anxieties and opinions still exist today, but they are no longer a central component of the ideology of European Christian Democracy. When old fears are expressed openly, as in Enoch Powell's remarks on the sanguinary consequences of differences in 'immigrant' and 'native' fertility rates, they are condemned today by conservatives whose predecessors would have adhered casually to more extreme views.

It is the contention of this paper, therefore, that the intellectual milieu which produced the fear of population decline in the period 1870–1940 had changed significantly in Europe by 1945. In the decade of decolonization and afterward, attention turned towards the menace of overpopulation, particularly in the Third World. It is highly unlikely that future discussions of population problems in Europe will be based on pre-1940 assumptions, but ideological concerns are bound to remain part of demographic debate.

It is surprising that so important a chapter in European intellectual history has yet to be written. The most useful previous studies, such as that of J. J. Spengler (1938), concentrate on the writings of economists and other social scientists. While it is of considerable interest to know how writing on population questions affected the development of economic thought and vice-versa, it is equally necessary to place the work of academics and other professional scholars in the context of a much wider body of opinion about population change. This paper is a preliminary attempt to do so, by introducing some of the main features of popular demographic arguments and by analysing briefly their appearance and disappearance in Europe over the past century.

There were two major aspects of the fear of population decline. They overlapped considerably, but for purposes of analysis they can be treated separately. One group of writers and politicians focused on what they took to be the deleterious consequences of aggregate population decline. Pro-natalists, particularly in France, were found both on the left and right of the European political spectrum. Many of them used the population factor to account for a whole range of past failures and to serve as the basis for predictions of future ones. Men of all political persuasions found in demographic arguments convenient explanations for phenomena which were capable of much simpler interpretation.

The mountain of literature produced on population questions in the period 1870–1940 included, as well, a large body of Malthusian writing. But many advocates of population control were worried about the implications of declining rates of population growth in one country but not in its neighbours. To some, depopulation was a form of unilateral disarmament, and therefore, inherently dangerous. The military significance of many Malthusian and anti-Malthusian arguments gave them an importance of which political leaders were aware.

A second group of writers were more concerned about the supposed implications of differential fertility rates as between classes. Here, the analogy between internal and international instability was made frequently by those who saw a common thread linking both levels of social conflict. The population question in internal politics cannot be divorced from its perceived significance in international affairs. In the aftermath of the Franco–Prussian War and the Paris Commune, and still more after the Russian Revolution, these two sets of anxieties reinforced each other and served to occasion an enormous literature on the likelihood and consequences of depopulation.

A preliminary word is necessary about the representativeness of the writers whose views are discussed in this paper. Some of them must be placed on what we call the lunatic fringe. Some others expressed a more common form of political commitment, which Richard Hofstadter (1965) called the 'paranoid style' of politics.

Many contradicted themselves and others of similar persuasion so frequently, that in no sense can the people whose ideas are examined below be described as forming a school of thought. But it would be wrong to dismiss all spokesmen of the fear of population decline as political fanatics in pseudo-scientific garb. Sober men from many walks of life contributed to the debate over demographic trends, which was not restricted to learned journals or societies. The mass circulation socialist newspaper, the *Daily Herald*, produced a banner headline on 3 November 1930 which announced: 'Fewer British Babies. Sudden Birth Slump. Population May Soon Become Stationary in Britain if Decline Lasts'. In France, the publication of census returns was the occasion for heated debate about what steps to take to ensure the future of the French nation. It is in the context of a widespread public discussion of population growth as an indicator of national or class vitality that one must set the writings analysed here.

In 1935, Gaston Bouthoul, Professor at the Ecole des Hautes Etudes Sociales in Paris and a specialist on population questions, succinctly summarized the character of much writing on the subject, including his own. Discussions of population dynamics, wrote Bouthoul, are frequently marred by the injection into them of 'preconceived ideas, and of preconceived political ideas above all. One could say that in France the vast majority of works bearing on population are forms of special pleading, speeches for the defence, more or less masked' (Bouthoul, 1937, p. 7). The content of that defence depended in large part on the perception of a threat to nation or to class which was expressed in demographic form. We can see the validity of Bouthoul's remarks by examining writings on population in Western Europe and by placing them in the contexts of military anxiety and class fears, which together fed apprehension about racial decline.

Demography and international politics

The military consequences of population movements were discussed incessantly from the time of the Franco–Prussian War until World War 2. The tone of much of this debate can be sensed from one of the earliest and most revealing statements linking war and population. Pierre Toulemont, a Jesuit priest, saw the débâcle of Napoleon III's military campaign and the spectre of the uprising and bloody suppression of the Paris Commune as signs of Divine chastisement of the French people for the sin of contraception (Toulemont 1872 and 1873, p. 511). The upsurge of pietism after the events of 1870–71, which has left as its monument the Basilica of Sacré Coeur in Montmartre (Gadille 1967, pp. 229 ff.), gave such statements a popular force at a time when Catholics and other French conservatives were unable to face more concrete explanations of the failures of their class and country.

German writers reinforced the urgency of attempts to explain, or rather to explain away, the sources of French weakness in European affairs, so blatantly demonstrated on the battlefields of Sedan. Typical of the brash chauvinism and hauteur of the spokesmen of the new Reich was the boast of the distinguished ancient historian, Theodor Mommsen, whose work on Rome gave him what was taken as a special insight into the character of declining, once glorious, powers. At Rome in 1878, Mommsen is reported to have said, 'Another German invasion, and all that will remain of France is a bad memory' (Bouthoul 1935, pp. 9–10).

The sentiment behind these inflated, and yet to the French sadly plausible, remarks was taken to heart by one of the most prolific writers on the military consequences of population decline, Paul Leroy-Beaulieu, Professor at the Collège de France and editor of L'économiste français. In 1881, he wrote in his journal that France must turn to colonial politics, since Continental politics were beyond the strength of her enfeebled people. 'It takes courage', he wrote,

> to tell the truth to one's own country and to destroy those illusions that will bring us new reverses and new catastrophes. In the presence of a Germany of 45 million inhabitants who will be 60 million in 20 years and 80 million in 50 years, and who can count on the loyalty of the Austrian populations, all the hopes of armed revenge are chimeras, sentimental and patriotic delusions, singularly dangerous for our country.

The annexation of Tunisia, he argued, was a step in the direction of national glory, more appropriate to France than a suicidal attempt to regain Alsace and Lorraine by force of arms (Leroy-Beaulieu 1881). In his review of the 1881 census, the French Minister of the Interior, M. Goblet, voiced similar fears of French weakness. As The Times (1883) of London put it, 'there are not wanting now

Frenchmen who look on the decreasing population as but one among many signs of national degeneracy, and are ready to exclaim hopelessly, ''Finis Galliae'''. Here we see one of the central confusions of the fear of population decline: the fallacious equation of declining rates of natural increase with declining total populations.

In all these counsels of gloom, we can observe as well the tendency to presume rather than to prove that causal connections exist between demographic and political change. In the period before the full mechanization of warfare, it was understandable that many people assumed that military strength meant numerical superiority. What is less defensible was the reduction of all major questions of international politics to the level of mere reflections of vital statistics. Even Arsène Dumont, an anti-clerical Republican demographer who shared few of Leroy-Beaulieu's conservative opinions, argued in 1890 that 'a nation must have a population dense enough to keep stable an equilibrium with her neighbours, . . . ' This France was unable to do, and as a result, the standard-bearer of Republicanism and free thought 'will be at the mercy of monarchical and reactionary Europe', so long as France suffers from the 'disease' of low natality (Dumont 1890, pp. 57, 64).

British observers drew similar conclusions. One writer commented in 1902 that 'France's old desire for revenge upon Germany has now probably lost much of its strength' because of her demographic weakness (Holt Schooling 1902). Perhaps he would have been closer to the mark if he had said that the national spirit was willing, but the national flesh was too weak. This was the essence of numerous remarks in the decade prior to World War 1. One alarmed Frenchman put the following words into the mouth of an unnamed German professor, who surveyed the provisional results of French population movements in 1907 and concluded: ' ''More coffins than cradles: this is the beginning of the end'' ' and again ' ''Finis Galliae. Thus disappear by their own fault people who tamper with the fundamental laws of life'' ' (Savant 1909). A similarly lugubrious message was stated by another observer obsessed by the links between demography and military affairs. 'Militarily speaking', A. de Foville wrote in 1909,

> we have an increase in feebleness which accounts for the growing scantiness of our annual conscription, while abundant reinforcements

build up in the armies in contrast to which we have been unable to keep
pace since 1870. That being so, what can our sons and grandsons hope
for in future conflicts, regardless of how valiant they may be?

It must have come as a great surprise to these prophets of doom
that Verdun held six years later and that virile Germany lost the war
of attrition on the Western Front. But the fact that France's population growth rates still lagged behind those of Germany in the
interwar years continued to trouble the victorious French. During
an election speech in 1924, the French Prime Minister, Poincaré,
drew the attention of the Congress of Republican Federations to
the 'military problems' which followed from demographic decline
(*The Times* 1924a). A writer in *Germania*, the journal of the
Catholic Centre Party, believed that this anxiety was the real source
of French revanchism and her general hostility over reparations
and the Rhineland (*The Times* 1924). Here again we see the need to
find a demographic explanation for international developments as
an alternative to simpler and more justifiable grounds for French
policies.

A good example of what may be termed the confusions of political demography emerged in a discussion of the French occupation
of the Rhineland in 1920, following the entry of German soldiers
into the Ruhr. What shocked many observers on the left as well as
on the right was the use of black Moroccan soldiers by the French
to police a white population. The press was replete with fears of
this unleashing of African sexuality on European womanhood
(Reinders 1968). But for our purposes, the most revealing comment
was that of a former Liberal Member of Parliament recruited to the
Labour party, Sir Leo Chiozza Money (1925, p. 89). He reasoned
that France's fall in native fertility explained her use of black
soldiers on the Rhine. 'What a mournful problem it is', he lamen-
ted, 'this of France believing herself forced to frame a great black
army in anticipation of the failure of her white manhood'.

Whether or not this was true, it would be interesting to explore
the question as to whether the French strategic decision of the mid-
1920s to retreat behind a Maginot line reflected their recognition
that Germany could not be kept weak, and that consequently
defiance had to give way to defensiveness. The extent to which her
Allies' perception of French strength was affected by concern over
her population growth is a theme which also needs investigation in

detail. But we can gauge its importance by a reflective article written, perhaps with Foreign Office assistance, by the Paris correspondent of *The Times* in early 1939. The writer saw in slow population growth the source of 'the paralysis of French initiative' and 'of the chronic depression from which she is suffering'. The reader might well have wondered why Britian should fight alongside such a decadent partner. Thus a demographic argument could be made out for appeasement, just as in the 1920s, a demographic explanation was offered for French intransigence and bellicosity.

The fall of France in 1940 provided another opportunity to account for political and military failures on demographic grounds. In a spirited call to Frenchmen to confront the population problem, which was 'for France, the essential problem, the only real problem', Robert Debré and Alfred Sauvy wrote in 1946 that

> The terrible failure of 1940, more moral than material, must be linked in part to this dangerous sclerosis [resulting from low birth rates]. We saw all too often, during the Occupation, old men leaning wearily towards the servile solution, at the time that the young were taking part in the national impulse towards independence and liberty. This crucial effect of our senility, is it not a grave warning?

For France, 'depopulation carried with it fatally a general legacy of decadence' made infinitely worse by the fact that the 'terrible ravages of the 1914–1918 war to the best of our men were not repaired'. This lowered 'the quality of leadership' in the interwar years (Debré and Sauvy 1946, pp. 9, 86). We shall return to this theme of a 'lost generation' of élites, as one of the pillars of the widespread fear of race suicide over which many Europeans brooded in the first half of this century.

Other European pessimists cast their nets further afield to find the link between population change and international politics. In Britain, concern over the tenuous hold of a 'declining race' over a far-flung Empire was a recurrent theme. As Arthur Newsholme (1906, pp. 57, 58), the Chief Medical Officer to the Local Government Board, put it:

> It cannot be regarded as a matter of indifference whether the unfilled portions of the world shall be peopled by Eastern races (Chinese, Japanese, Hindoos etc.), by Negroes, by Sclavonic [sic] or other Eastern European peoples, by the Latin races, or by the races of Eastern Europe.

'Every Briton', he assumed, 'will wish that his race may have a predominant share in shaping the future destinies of mankind'. Montague Crackanthorpe (1906), a conservative eugenist, drew the parallel between the decline of natality in Rome and in Britain, and with Gibbon, cried, 'Outraged Nature will have her revenges'. Dampier Whetham (1917, p. 230), an economist who was an equally conservative exponent of eugenics, voiced the standard pro-natalist claim, with a eugenic gloss, in a review of the rise of marriage and birth rates in the first year of the Great War. In his view, these increases showed a quickened sense of patriotism in the British population, who recognized that 'the welfare of the country and the Empire depends on an adequate supply of satisfactory men and women, . . . ' In a similar vein, he had praised German strength before the war, which was 'ultimately owing to the fact that her birth rate did not begin to fall systematically till twenty years later than that of Great Britain, . . . ' And even then, in Germany that decline had 'not yet destroyed the old predominance of the stronger and more intellectual sections of the nation', who were the vanguard of an Imperial race (Whetham and Whetham 1909, pp. 131–3).

The same theme of Imperial defence lay behind the establishment under the auspices of the National League of Life of an unofficial National Birth-rate Commission, which met intermittently between 1913 and 1926. The leading spirit behind its work was the Rev. James Marchant (1917, pp. 10, 17), a confirmed pro-natalist, who summarized its mixture of military and Imperial themes in a 1917 pamphlet. From the answer to the rhetorical question, 'would Germany have declared war on France if her population had been as large as Germany's?', he inferred that 'In the difference between the number of coffins and the number of cradles lies the existence and persistence of our Empire'.

In the same year that Marchant wrote, the Russian Revolution added a new dimension and a new level of hysteria to the fear of population decline in Western Europe. In 1920, Sir Rider Haggard, a novelist and vice-president of the Royal Colonial Institute, warned that unless Russian numbers were diminished, 'directed by German skill and courage and aided by other sinister influences, what devastation might they not work upon the rest of Europe, should its manpower be depleted' (Marchant 1920, p. 180). Chiozza Money saw the revolution spreading in several directions at once. In China as elsewhere, he noted in 1925 (pp. 78, 96 and 97) 'we have to reckon with the Bolshevist menace. The Soviet agents, emissaries as deadly as any dispatched of old by the sect of assassins, work eagerly to foment disorder, to make China a determining factor in world revolution'. And what is worse, 'we have to consider the influence of Bolshevism in a world in which White Civilization is sufficiently in danger' without it, because of declining fertility. The same fear troubled C. P. Blacker, an active member of the Eugenics Society. In 1926, the year of the General Strike in Britain, Blacker wrote of the danger of the spread of Communism in the aftermath of the Bolshevik Revolution, that 'event which in 1917 cast her beyond the pale of Western Civilization'. Should another world war break out, the British Empire would have no hope of survival. Furthermore, 'The seeds of revolution in Europe, by then more deeply sown, would germinate, and the present social order would come to an end' (Blacker 1926, pp. 72, 76–8). In 1934, a Swiss economist of Hungarian origin wrote that 'we must take note of the risk of another great Western invasion of the peoples of the East', whose inferior living conditions would impel them westward (Ferenczi 1934). He neglected to mention that, whatever other problems Russians faced in the early 1930s, the terrible dislocation associated with the world economic crisis was not one of them. After World War 2, a leading Catholic pro-natalist, Halliday Sutherland (1951, p. 33), took up the by then familiar theme. In the Soviet Union, he noted, there was 'an enormous population which might easily overflow into the underpopulated lands of the less virile races. These towering facts make one wonder how any government in Western Europe could be so senseless as to tolerate the preaching of contraception'.

All the above writings, it must be recalled, appeared in books and articles devoted ostensibly to the study of population questions. The Italian and German fascists had, of course, an enormous battery of 'evidence' justifying on demographic grounds the oppression of inferior races at home and of lesser races abroad (Kuczynski 1939 and Gini 1923, pp. 430–1). But as we have seen, they were certainly not alone in the use of demographic argument in the course of military and strategic discussions.

Demography and the defence of inequality

When we turn to population decline as a theme in discussions of internal politics, we see two related but not identical fears expressed by men of the right. The first is anxiety over the eclipse of élites by the more prolific masses. The second is worry over pollution of the white race by miscegenation. While most defenders of social inequality in Europe and America were also racialists, the converse is not strictly true. The reason is that the anti-elitism of National Socialism separated it from the ideology of many of its conservative allies. The Nazis argued that Aryan features and pure blood were the essence of the *Volk*, and not the monopoly of any one class. For this and other reasons, the place of traditional élites in the Nazi state was precarious, as many of them recognized belatedly. Fears of social submergence and racial decline frequently coincided, but were not totally fused.

This is not to deny the affinity between some sources of fascist thinking and the views of conservative exponents of the fear of population decline, taken as the decline of élites. Consider the book on heredity and society written by Dampier Whetham, the Cambridge economist, and his wife in 1912. The Whethams had just read Houston Stewart Chamberlain's book, *The Foundations of the Nineteenth Century*, which later became a minor classic of Nazi 'thought'. At a time of unprecedented labour unrest, and during the controversy over the restriction of the veto power of the House of Lords, the Whethams found Chamberlain's views to be profoundly important. What he had done, in their opinion, was to show that

> The great things of the world are accomplished by individuals who have a strong personality and by races which have a strong race-personality. Within a nation itself, the best work is done by groups or sections of the people that are easily recognized and have strongly marked characteristics. We have shown reason to believe that this differentiation of type into so-called classes, which is found in all successful national evolution, is essential to the maintenance of progress.

But with the full flavour of the pessimism of élites under siege, they feared for the future of England. Why? Because in their day

> Great men are scarce; the group personality is becoming indistinct and the personality of the race by which success was attained in the past, is therefore on the wane, while the forces of chaos are once more being manufactured in our midst, ready to break loose and destroy the

civilization when the higher types are no longer sufficient in numbers
and effectiveness to guide, control, or subdue them (Whetham and
Whetham 1912, pp. 69–70).

Here we can see encapsulated the mixture of fear of social unrest
and the sense of a loss of mastery which marked the writings of
eugenists and others concerned with population decline. We can
also see how relatively lower fertility among élites, compared with
that of working people, provided such writers with a useful account
of their own apparent demise. If contraception, and not class
oppression or social injustice, was at the root of their trouble, then
no one in particular was to blame. Consequently for such writers,
demographic analysis conveniently and completely could displace
social analysis.

In this regard, consider the case of a British doctor and polemi-
cist, J. W. Taylor, who wrote in 1906 of the fact that the 'vicious
and unnatural habits of the present generation' had led to a dearth
of 'men of surpassing genius'. Oblivious of the contemporary existence of Picasso, Freud, or Einstein, Taylor concluded that 'Our
mischievous meddling with great natural forces' had stripped the
world of genius which, as in the cases of Shakespeare, Walter
Scott, and John Wesley, occurred in births of high rank order
(Taylor 1906, p. 226).

During World War 1, and in its aftermath, this theme of the
dearth of ability was transformed into the cult of the 'Lost Generation', the remembrance of social élites that fell in the war (Winter,
1977a). One of the more eccentric, but direct, links between the
fear of population decline and war losses was made by the anony-
mous medical writer who noted that one-child privileged families
who had lost their only sons in the war had been punished for their
'loathsome practices' and for following 'the foul teaching of family
limitation'(anon. 1917). Dr Caleb Saleeby, a Scotch physician and
eugenist, provided this visual record of the dysgenic character of
the war:

> Every afternoon when my work is done I go into Hyde Park, and I
> watch a small portion of Kitchener's Army drilling, and I compare
> those splendid young men, everyone of whom I pay homage in my
> heart, with the washouts, dirty, drunken, and diseased, whom no
> recruiting sergeant since time began wanted to look at a second time,
> lying about in the grass, and I realize the trash is remaining at home
> and the treasure is going away to be killed.

The very least England could do, he went on, was to protect the issue of the nation's 'treasure' by supporting soldiers' and sailors' wives who were pregnant and thereby were doing 'equally good service for England' by giving birth to a healthy new generation of future recruits (Saleeby 1914, pp. 5, 7). Perhaps this variant of the old adage, 'Lie back and think of England' can be traced, like so many other things, to World War 1.

Pro-natalists were not alone in stressing the need to procreate ability, or in so many words, to reproduce their own kind. Marie Stopes, the pioneer of birth-control clinics, told the National Birth-rate Commission that she wanted to increase the birth-rate among the 'better classes', because, 'In our class the children of the last twenty-five years are mentally and physically superior to those of the poorer and more thriftless of the working class' (Marchant, 1920, pp. 253, 255). The same opinion was voiced a few years later by Lucien March, president of the French Eugenics Society. He told an International Eugenics Conference in New York that 'innate qualities' were greater in large income families than in poorer families (March 1923, pp. 249–250). In 1930, a British biologist, R. A. Fisher, who later held the Chair of Eugenics in London and the Chair of Genetics in Cambridge, added his weight to the argument that 'a number of qualities of moral character' showed 'a relative concentration in the more prosperous strata of existing populations' (Fisher, 1930, pp. 262–3). Leonard Darwin, fourth son of Charles Darwin, and President of the Eugenics Society, concurred on a number of occasions (Darwin, 1926, p. 327 and 1928, p. 67). C. P. Blacker made the similar claim in 1934 that those who 'rise in the social scale exhibit socially valuable qualities which are largely innate and at least partly hereditary' (Blacker, 1934, p. 74). Two years previously, a German biologist made the same assertion. The 'catastrophic fall' in European fertility was, in his view, bound to 'reduce considerably the number of stocks which carry on to posterity the national heritage' (Fischer 1932, p. 105).

The social prejudices in favour of élites produced equally distorted views of the supposed biological flaws inherent in large sections of the mass of the population. A Liverpool physician, R. R. Rentoul, was convinced that people who lived in slums were predisposed hereditarily to do so (Rentoul 1906, p. xii). In 1906, one of

Karl Pearson's associates at University College, London published a learned study of fertility and social status, the purpose of which was to demonstrate the 'very close relationship between undesirable social status and a high birth rate'. General labourers and other 'mentally and physically feebler stocks' were reproducing themselves at much greater rates than were professionals and other 'abler and more capable stocks' (Heron 1906, p. 21).

Discussions of welfare measures and how to pay for them brought out more extreme statements. Even though there was no rigorous definition of who might be termed 'feeble-minded', this did not prevent eugenists from referring to them as 'the kith and kin of the epileptic, the insane and mentally unstable, the criminal, the chronic pauper and unemployable classes', the support of whom was bound to 'impede national advance' (Tredgold 1910). The country could not 'preserve and multiply these weaklings in mind', wrote Leonard Huxley, the son and biographer of T. H. Huxley, since they 'make the nation incurably below C3', that is, below the mental equivalent of the minimum standard for induction into the army (Huxley 1926, p. 38).

On a more general level, Leonard Darwin wrote in 1917 that public assistance of any kind, while soothing to humanitarian sentiment, was undoubtedly dysgenic. The appearance of such 'Civilizing influences' in the past may help to 'explain why ancient civilizations have often died out' (Darwin 1917). Fifteen years later, at the height of the world economic crisis, R. Ruggles Gates, Professor of Botany at King's College, London, told the Centenary Meeting of the British Association that public support of working-class nutrition and health was positively harmful. 'The view that populations exist as blind mouths to be fed and educated regardless of their racial worth is all too prevalent and will lead us along the road to racial decay' (Gates 1932). A general summary of these ruminations on population decline and welfare may be found in the following remarks of Professor G. N. de Lapouge, Professor of Anthropology in the University of Montpellier, to the 1921 International Eugenics Conference. 'The time has come', he insisted,

> when man must choose whether he will be a demi-god or whether he will turn to barbarism. And this is not a figure of speech. The less well-endowed classes, the residue of 'uncivilizables', reproach their superiors for having created a civilization which multiplies their desires beyond the possibility of their satisfaction. An immense

movement has started among races and inferior classes, and this
movement which can be turned against the white race, is turned also
against intellectually superior elements and against civilization itself.
Class war is the real race war (de Lapouge 1923).

The sources of racialism cannot be traced to the fear of population decline, but the equation of race war and class war had an
ominous significance to many who expressed these anxieties. Given
the legacy of slavery, it is not surprising that Americans used population questions to express fears somewhat different from those of
their European contemporaries. The European fear of the lower
orders had a partial equivalent in the American obsession with
blacks and with the immigrants from Eastern and Southern
Europe, who brought with them what were seen as unamerican
habits and unamerican ideas. These aspects of 'alien behaviour'
became fused and magnified after the Russian Revolution. Consider the welcoming remarks of Henry Fairfield Osborn of the
American Museum of Natural History to delegates to the 1921
International Eugenics Conference. He told delegates that 'In
certain parts of Europe the worst elements of society have gained
the ascendancy and threaten the destruction of the best'. With
proper immigration controls, no such threat would materialize in
America, he presumed (Osborn, 1923). Once again, we can see
how inextricably linked were international and internal concerns
in the minds of those who wrote about population earlier in this
century. ·

   Many of the other delegates to this conference were particularly
interested in the demographic and social significance of race. For
the occasion, an exhibition was prepared, many of the displays of
which presented 'scientific proof' of the innate inferiority of
Negroes. How pervasive such ideas were may be seen in the following discussion of race in the course of a book by an American
academic writer on population questions, Professor Edward M.
East of Harvard. In 1920, he advanced the 'theory' that

> The Negro is a happy-go-lucky child, naturally expansive under simple
> conditions; oppressed by the restriction of civilization. He accepts his
> limitation; indeed he is rather glad to have them. Only when there is
> white blood in his veins does he cry out against the supposed injustice
> of his condition.

The particular mulatto he had in mind was the distinguished black
scholar W. E. B. Dubois (East 1920 and 1923, p. 119). East seems

to have been unaware that very few American blacks were of what he referred to as pure African 'stock'.

European writers of the same generation were not free of similar, and at times equally virulent, strains of racial prejudice, which infused the second aspect of the fear of population decline, as racial decay from within. One of the most extreme cases was that of the Liverpool physician Rentoul. 'The inter-marriage of Britons with foreigners', he counselled, 'should not be encouraged. A few of us know the terrible monstrosities produced by the inter-marriage of the white man and the black, the white man with the redskin, the white man with the native Hindu, or the white man with the Chinese'. In phrases that would have warmed the heart of Himmler, Rentoul gave full vent to his fantasies. 'The Negro is seldom content with sexual intercourse with the white woman, but culminates his sexual furore by killing the woman, sometimes taking out her womb and eating it' (Rentoul 1906, p. 31). Somewhat less hysterical, but equally infused with prejudice, was the remark of Caleb Saleeby that 'the child of the lower races degenerates at puberty'. He followed this statement with a surrealistic description of non-white cranial physiology (Saleeby 1921, p. 61). In another context, Dr Saleeby ridiculed the work of a contemporary who 'would almost have us believe that the Negro is mentally and morally the equal of the Caucasian' (Saleeby 1909, p. xi). J. S. Huxley held similar views. He opposed miscegenation on the grounds that society had to avoid a 'large proportion of disharmonic combinations' (Huxley 1926). Lucien March said that the French faced just such a fate as a result of the immigration of 'unassimilable races . . . which will quickly furnish undesirable elements' (March, 1923, p. 251). These statements are but the tip of the iceberg of endemic racial prejudice in Western Europe in the period under review. A mere glance at the literature on population questions will suffice to show that there was nothing specifically German in the blend of racial theory concocted by fascists and their fellow travellers in the 1920s and 1930s.

On other grounds, some eugenists, such as the Oxford philosopher F. C. S. Schiller, openly expressed their sympathies with fascism and other reactionary movements. To such men, they constituted the most effective anti-socialist weapon, worthy of support because socialism was 'an unintelligent attempt to equalize human conditions without regard to mind or capacity, which is inspired mainly by envy and sentimentalism' (Schiller 1932, p. 8 and Abel 1955, pp. 146–7). Halliday Sutherland, a well-known Catholic crusader against contraception, was invited to Spain by the Franco government in 1946. The next year he reminisced about his trip and wrote a defence of Franco and a sympathetic appraisal of the ideology of Antonio Primo de Rivera, the founder of the Falangist movement (Sutherland 1947). Sutherland's mixture of Catholicism and anti-communism (Sutherland 1936, pp. 235–6) was less prevalent in Britain than in France, where socialist anti-clericalism offended many religiously-inclined exponents of the fear of population decline. The power of the extreme right in France before 1940 was reflected in the deeply conservative character of much French writing on population problems during the Third Republic.

Social democracy and population decline

In the light of such right-wing views, it is remarkable how widely shared by the left were general fears of population decline in Europe in this period. What could socialists and radical liberals have in common with the views of conservatives, such as Dr C. M. Burns, who, in a book on infant and maternal mortality published in 1942, called for a reduction of 'the flotsam in future generations' not by social reform but by better breeding? After all, she noted, 'The black spot cannot be "bred out" of a terrier's litter by merely giving the mother a good kennel' (Burns 1942, p. 246). It is obvious that this sort of negative eugenics was repugnant to men and women of the left, who were prepared, nonetheless, to argue that aggregate population growth had to be kept up in order to assure the future of social democracy in Europe.

Richard and Kathleen Titmuss expressed one version of this argument when they asserted in 1942 that an ageing population is more interested in security than in reform. A declining rate of population growth, therefore, meant that 'society will lose the mental attitude that is essential for social progress. . . . ' They admitted that an ageing population was one 'ripe [in] experience and Victorian memories', but added these questions: 'are these the gifts we require to build a New Social Order? If this age structure explains in part our shortcomings during the past ten years will it not also shape our future; a cautious, timid, benevolent' future, perhaps, but not a socialist one? (Titmuss and Titmuss 1942, pp. 42, 47). Here again we find a partial demographic explanation of political failure, this time of the left, when a survey of economic conditions alone could account for many of the setbacks of the left in the 1930s.

The Titmusses formulated, as well, a second aspect of the socialist analysis of population decline. On the assumption that 'Man's attitude to the reproduction of his own species is the key to all other problems', they concluded that declining fertility was an indictment of capitalism on the part of people who did not want to bring children into the world it had created. The ethical socialism of R. H. Tawney is clear in the following summary statement of this position: 'So long as men, twisting, turning, fighting, and rolling in an economic society, in which they are saturated with class thinking, are forced to compete one with another, so long will they refuse to reproduce themselves' (Titmuss and Titmuss, 1942, pp. 31, 116). The social biologist Lancelot Hogben concurred. 'The population crisis to which urban civilization is now heading', he wrote in 1936, 'is the biological proof of its inadequacy' (Hogben 1936, p. 50). Enid Charles, the author of The Menace of Under-Population, and Hogben's wife, wrote similarly that the 'ultimate condemnation' of capitalism, or (borrowing from Tawney again) of the Acquisitive Society, 'is that it has now ceased to be able to accommodate the biological machinery by which any form of society can be perpetuated' (Charles 1936, p. 223). The assumption of many of these writers, with the exception of the agnostic and iconoclastic Hogben, was that a socialist society would be a more fertile one (Hogben 1937, p. 178).

Liberal economists avoided similar indictments of capitalism, but many of them were worried about the consequences of the slowdown of rates of population growth. J. A. Hobson, a member of the National Birth-rate Commission, found the discussion of population decline perfectly compatible with his under-consumptionist theories (Marchant 1920). J. M. Keynes, in the late 1930s, advanced the view that the recovery of fertility rates would help stimulate aggregate demand and replenish sources of capital (Keynes 1937). Sir William Beveridge, his biographer tells us, derived his concern about the limitation of fertility from three sources:

firstly, from a fear of the ultimate eclipse of the most 'advanced' races; secondly, from a desire to avoid producing a society over- loaded with old people; and thirdly, from a belief that birth control was mainly practiced by the most 'responsible' sections of society and might therefore be harming the 'national stock' (Harris 1977, p. 342).

These sentiments were enshrined in the Beveridge Report of 1942, wherein family allowances and maternal welfare provision were defended on the grounds that women 'have vital work to do in insuring the adequate continuance of the British race and British ideals in the world'.

Beveridge's ideas on population questions bring out many of the reasons why social reformers' fears of population decline were so similar to those of their political opponents. Firstly, Beveridge and Sidney Webb, to take two of the most prominent progressive expo- nents of these anxieties, were strongly influenced both by positivism and by the work of Francis Galton. To them fertility was a social fact whose laws could be ascertained by appropriate study. The science of population change was bound to have an attraction for them, as it did for men of very different political views. Secondly, Beveridge and Webb epitomized in their work and thought a form of bureaucratic liberalism and bureaucratic social- ism which coincided at many points. To men who shared their administrative cast of mind, fertility was but one aspect of human behaviour which, like most others, could be, and ought to be, regu- lated in the national interest. Thirdly, this form of collectivism was the doctrine of professional men and women, who had little direct contact with the working class, opposed strategies of class struggle, and expressed at times strong disapproval of the poorest sections of society. A belief in equality was not at the centre of their political philosophy, a fact which may help to account for their inability to overcome the racial prejudices of the day (Winter 1974, Ch. 2). Fourthly, both Beveridge and Webb were consummate oppor- tunists who used the spectre of population decline to frighten politi- cians who needed a reason to press on with reform. A mixture of philanthropy and patriotism, fuelled by concern over population growth, did much to advance the cause of welfare legislation in Western Europe in this century. In campaigns in Britain and France on behalf of maternal and infant health we can see strange bed- fellows dwelling together whose only common idea was anxiety over fertility limitation (Winter 1977b). Similarly, the call for a reduction of school fees rested in part on the assumption that they were responsible for 'the toll . . . which is at present extracted from our birth-rate' (Leybourne and White 1940, p. 324). Demographic arguments once again came in handy in battles for social reform.

Finally, the socialist and social democratic advocacy of the fear of population decline makes most sense as an expression of the deep patriotism of the West European left. The national consciousness of the French left drew on memories of the *levée en masse* of the Revolutionary and Napoleonic periods and of the heroic resistance to enemies foreign and domestic of the Paris Commune. Its force can be felt in the surge of mass enthusiasm for war in August 1914. In Britain the call for the defence of Empire and nation drew the same overwhelming response. Working-class patriotism did not abate in the interwar years. In this period, too, it was with some justification that socialists in Britain identified the future of their cause with the future of their own country. Since social democracy had collapsed everywhere else in Europe between 1919 and 1940, its existence would be assured, many believed, only if Britain remained healthy and strong. For this reason, men on the left felt that they had cause for concern over declining rates of population growth which were, in their view, incompatible with national vitality.

Conclusion

We have seen that there were two principal aspects of the fear of population decline: the first concerned general fertility levels; the second concerned variations in the fertility rates of specific social groups. After World War 2, both fears receded, and anxiety over differential fertility was largely discredited. The recognition of the consequences of the application of racial theories to the 'final solution of the Jewish problem' made it impossible to use in civilized discourse the language of animal breeding so prevalent in population debate earlier in the century.

The war transformed the political atmosphere in which population questions were discussed. Burdened with the legacy of collaboration, the radical right was eclipsed for a time, and into obscurity with it went much of the chauvinistic advocacy of natality on military or class lines. Bolstered by the crucial role played by Communists and Socialists in the resistance to Hitler, the left gained the ground lost by the right, and won the support of many who simply had no wish to return to the social conditions of the Conservative-dominated Europe in the 1930s. As the conditions of political conflict changes, so the language of social conflict changed with them. As a consequence, there were few echoes after 1945 of the need to sterilize the unfit, the undesirable, or the unemployed, or to maximize the fertility of the élites. In addition, the advocates of the view that wealth and innate ability were linked genetically never recovered from the shock of the Depression. In the period surrounding World War 2 many of the advocates of measures to change the social balance of fertility abandoned their earlier views. Others retained them, but lapsed into uncomfortable silence.

Their silence can be traced as well to the fact that even before the war, many of the scientific arguments used to justify the restriction of the fertility of certain classes had been rejected by scientists themselves. Once the transmission of diseases by carriers of recessive genes was firmly established, the idea of controlling what were deemed hereditary diseases by sterilization of those who suffered from them, was shown to be ineffective and dangerous nonsense. Furthermore, advances in pathology, psychiatry, and epidemiology precluded the perpetuation of many earlier claims that certain diseases, such as tuberculosis, or certain neurotic conditions were inherited, or that they were merely symptoms of 'damaged germ plasm'. Similarly, advances in the study of mutations discredited any version of the theory of the survival of the fittest, however defined (Hogben 1934, and Muller 1936, p. 51).

With some justification, biologists like Lancelot Hogben ridiculed those worried about the proliferating unfit, not because such eugenists emphasized the need to study genetics, but because they were profoundly ignorant of the supposed scientific basis of their views (Hogben 1931, pp. 99, 209, 211). The advocates of eugenics could not easily dismiss the opinion of scientists who argued that before we could know whether human attributes or abilities were inherited, and if so to what degree, social conditions would have to be equalized (Haldane 1938, p. 112). The essential problem of eugenics was that biology had passed it by.

Finally, the fact that the postwar baby boom lasted longer than anyone had predicted made it seem that somehow all the fuss over fertility had achieved results, and that therefore, old warriors could rest content. Had total fertility in the mid-1950s been as low as it was in the mid-1930s, it is possible that the fear of aggregate population decline would have continued to plague discussions of social policy. In recent years, a declining population has become for the first time a real possibility in Western Europe. Consequently, there has been a mild recrudescence of concern on the right over low natality. At the 1977 Gaullist party conference, the distinguished historian Pierre Chaunu warned his audience of the dire consequences to France and to the whole industrial world of the 'contraceptive revolution'. His country, he said, had not more than ten years to avoid disaster. Michel Debré, a still powerful figure in the party, reiterated the old call for 'a rejuvenated France' (*The Times,* 1977). Is it an accident that such fears were expressed at a time when the election of a Communist-Socialist coalition government in France was distinctly possible? How deeply felt today are such fears about population decline as political or social decline is a question which requires further investigation. But we should not be surprised if the subject of population still brings out the fears and hopes of contemporaries; for it has done so for as long a men have been aware of its existence.

Acknowledgement

Thanks are due to Dr Michael Teitelbaum and Professor Volker Berghahn for their advice on this paper.

References

ABEL, R. (1955) *The Pragmatic Humanism of F. C. S. Schiller* (New York: King's Crown Press).

ANON. (1917) War and population. *Journal of Tropical Medicine and Hygiene,* **20,** 238.

ANON. (1923) *The Second International Exhibition of Eugenics*, p. 108, on the less developed 'brain part' of Negro skulls and p. 120, on Negro mental fatigue. Anti-immigrant displays were also prepared. (Baltimore: Williams & Wilkins).

BLACKER, C. P. (1926) *Birth Control and the State* (London: E. P. Dutton & Co.).

BLACKER, C. P. (1934) *Voluntary Sterilization.* (London: Oxford University Press.

BOUTHOUL, G. (1935) *La population dans le monde.* (Paris: Payot).

BURNS, C. M. (1942) *Infant and Maternal Mortality in Relation to Size of Family* and *Rapidity of Breeding* (Newcastle-upon-Tyne: University of Durham College of Physical Science).

CHARLES, E. (1936) *The Menace of Under-population, a Biological Study of the Decline of Population Growth* (London: Watts & Co.).

CHIOZZA MONEY, L. (1925) *The Peril of the Whites* (London: Collins).

CRACKANTHORPE, M. (1906) Population and progress. *Fortnightly Review,* **86,** 1009.

DARWIN, L. (1917) The racial effects of public assistance. *Charity Organization Review,* **267,** 62.

DARWIN, L. (1926) *The Need for Eugenic Reform* (London: John Murray).

DARWIN, L. (1928) *What is Eugenics?* (London: Watts & Co.).

DEBRÉ, R. and SAUVY, A. (1946) *Des français pour la France. Le problème de la population* (Paris: Gallimard).

DUMONT, A. (1890) *Dépopulation et civilisation. Étude démographique* (Paris: Lecrosnier et Babé).

EAST, E. M. (1920) Population. *Scientific Monthly,* **10,** 621.

EAST, E. M. (1923) *Mankind at the Crossroads* (New York: Scribners).

FERENCZI, D. (1934) La politique économique mondiale et les changements dans la population. *Revue économique internationale,* **2,** 368.

FISCHER, E. (1932). Report on Meckermann's studies of the differential fertility within certain social groups in Germany. In *Problems of Population,* Pitt-Rivers, G. (ed.), p. 105 (London: George Allen & Unwin).

FISHER, R. A. (1930) *The Genetical Theory of Natural Selection.* (Oxford: Clarendon Press).

FOVILLE, A. de (1909) Enquête sur le dépeuplement de la France. *La revue hebdomadaire,* **5,** 7–8.

GADILLE, J. (1967) *La pensée et l'action politique des évêques français au début de la IIIe République,* vol. II (Paris: Hachette).

GATES, R. R. (1932) Eugenics and education. *Eugenics Review,* **23,** 307. See also the editorial 'Notes of the Quarter' on p. 199 of this journal, for an indictment of the wastefulness of social welfare provision.

GINI, C. (1923) The War from the Eugenic point of view. In *Eugenics in Race and State,* pp. 430–1 (Baltimore: Williams & Wilkins).

HALDANE, J. B. S. (1938) *Heredity and Politics* (London: George Allen & Unwin).

HARRIS, J. (1977) *William Beveridge. A Biography.* (Oxford: Oxford University Press).

HERON, D. (1906) *On the Relation of Fertility in Man to Social Status, and on the Changes in the Relation that have Taken Place during the Last Fifty Years.* Drapers Co. Research Memoirs Studies in National Deterioration I, p. 21 (London: Dulau & Co.).

HOFSTADTER, R. (1965) *The Paranoid Style in American Politics, and Other Essays* (New York: Knopf).

HOGBEN, L. (1931) *Genetic Principles in Medicine and Social Science* (London: Williams & Norgate).

HOGBEN, L. (1934) Heredity and human affairs. In *Science To-day,* Thomson, J. A. (ed.), pp. 25–6 (London: Eyre & Spottiswoode).

HOGBEN, L. (1936) *The Retreat from Reason* (London: Watts & Co.).

HOGBEN, L. (1937) Planning for human survival. In *What is Ahead of Us?* Cole, G. D. H. (ed.), p. 178 (London: Macmillan).

HOLT SCHOOLING, J. (1902) The natural increase of three populations. *Contemporary Review,* **81,** 232, 237.

HUXLEY, J. S. (1926) *Biology and Human Life.* 2nd Norman Lockyer Lecture, p. 21 (London: British Science Guild).

HUXLEY, L. (1926) *Progress and the Unfit* (London: Watts & Co.).

KEYNES, J. M. (1937) The economic consequences of a declining population. *Eugenics Review,* **29,** 13–17.

KUCZYNSKI, R. R. (1939) *'Living Space' and Population Problems* (Oxford: Clarendon Press).

LAPOUGE, G. DE (1923) La race chez les populations melangées. In *Eugenics in Race and State* (Baltimore: Williams & Wilkins).

LEROY-BEAULIEU, P. (1881) La politique continentale et la politique coloniale. *L'économiste français.*

LEYBOURNE, G. and WHITE, K. (1940) *Education and the Birth Rate.* (London: Jonathan Cape).

MARCH, L. (1923) The consequences of war on the birth rate in France. In *Eugenics, Genetics and the Family.* Osborne, H. (ed.) (Baltimore, Williams & Wilkins).

MARCHANT, J. (1917) *Cradles or Coffins.* National Life Series No. 2. (London: Chapman & Hall).

MARCHANT, J. (ed.) (1920) *Problems of Population and Parenthood* (London: Chapman & Hall).

MULLER, H. J. (1936) *Out of the Night. A Biologist's View of the Future* (London: Gollancz).

NEWSHOLME, A. (1906) *The Declining Birth Rates: its National and International Significance* (London: Cassell).

OSBORN, H. (1923) Opening remarks. In *Eugenics, Genetics and the Family* (Baltimore: Williams & Wilkins).

REINDERS, R. C. (1968) Racialism on the Left: E. D. Morel and the 'Black Horror on the Rhine'. *International Review of Social History,* **1,** 28.

RENTOUL, R. R. (1906) *Race Culture or Race Suicide?,* p. xii (London: Walter Scott Publishing Co.).

ROBERTS, J. M. (1973) *The Paris Commune from the Right.* (London: Longman).

SALEEBY, C. (1909) *Parenthood and Race Culture.* p. xi, (London: Cassell).

SALEEBY, C. (1914) *War and Waste.* (Manchester).

SALEEBY, C. (1921) *The Eugenic Prospect* (London: T. Fisher Unwin).

SAVANT, C.-M. (1909) La dépeuplement de la France. *La revue hebdomadaire,* **2,** 242.

SCHILLER, F. C. S. (1932) *Social Decay and Eugenic Reform* (London: Constable).

SPENGLER, J. (1938) *France Faces Depopulation* (Durham, North Carolina: North Carolina University Press).

SUTHERLAND, H. (1936) *In my Path* (London: Geoffrey Bles).

SUTHERLAND, H. (1947) Communists and Spain. *The Month,* **183,** 83, 92–3.

SUTHERLAND, H. (1951) *Control of Life.* 5th edn (London: Burns Oates).

TAYLOR, J. W. (1906) The Bishop of London and the declining birth rate. *Nineteenth Century,* **59,** 226.

The Times (1883) Decay of population in France. January 16.

The Times (1924a) French Government's programme. April 25.

The Times (1924b) Franco-German relations. January 26.

The Times (1939) The Family in France. January 16.

The Times (1977) Gaullists lectured on the dangers of decline in birth rate. September 29.

TITMUSS, R. and TITMUSS, K. (1942) *Parents Revolt* (London: Secker & Warburg).

TOULEMONT, Le P. P. (1872) *La Providence et les châtiments de la France* (Paris: J. Albanel).

TOULEMONT, Le P. P. (1873) *Un grand mal social* (Lyon: Pitrat aîné).
TREDGOLD, A. (1910) The feeble-minded. *Contemporary Review,* **97**, 720
WHETHAM, W. C. D. and WHETHAM, C. D. (1909) *The Family and the Nation: A Study of Natural Inheritance and Social Responsibility* (London: Longman).
WHETHAM, W. C. D. and WHETHAM, C. D. (1912) *Heredity and Society* (London: Longman).
WHETHAM, W. C. D. (1917) *The War and the Nation: A Study of Constructive Politics* (London: John Murray).
WINTER, J. M. (1974) *Socialism and the Challenge of War* (London: Routledge & Kegan Paul).
WINTER, J. M. (1977a) Britain's 'Lost Generation' of the First World War. *Population Studies,* **31**, 449–466.
WINTER, J. M. (1977b) The impact of the First World War on civilian health in Britain. *Economic History Review,* **30**, 487–504.

AUTHOR INDEX

Bold numerals indicate a paper in this volume

SUBJECT INDEX